IN THE BL

IN THE BLACK

LIVE FAITHFULLY, PROSPER FINANCIALLY

The Ultimate 9-Step Plan for Financial Fitness

AARON W. SMITH

with Brenda Lane Richardson

Amistad
An Imprint of HarperCollins *Publishers*

HARPER

HarperCollins books may be purchased for educational, business, or sales promotional use. For information please write: Special Markets Department, HarperCollins Publishers, 10 East 53rd Street, New York, NY 10022.

FIRST EDITION

Designed by Sara Maya Gubkin

Library of Congress Cataloging-in-Publication Data has been applied for.

ISBN 978-0-06-145069-3

09 10 11 12 13   WBC/RRD 10 9 8 7 6 5 4 3 2 1

Contents

Step 4: Quit Strumming the Money Blues

Step 5: Put the Pieces Together

Step 6: View Home Ownership as a Viable Option

Step 7: Don't Just Play the Market, Understand It

Step 8: Protect Your Assets

Step 9: Enjoy the Richness of Your Life

Acknowledgments

From Aaron Smith:

I want to thank Patricia, my wife, for her commitment to our financial business, to this book, and even more so, to me and our family. Her commitment to God has shaped who she is as a wife, friend, and mother. She is a wonderful asset to my life, to our children, and to this work, and I thank God for her.

I have learned also from our children, Jasmine K. Smith and Aaron Justin Smith, that our time together is far more valuable than anything that can be found in a bank. That has made me a stronger financial adviser.

As always, I am grateful to my parents, Johnnie E. Smith and Louise A. Smith. They provided a strong church foundation and were always there for our family. They supported us in every way, including our academic and athletic involvements, both of which have gotten me where I am today.

My pastor, the Reverend Andrew Mosley, Sr., encouraged me to think broadly by teaching me that there are two sides to any argument and helped me to look beyond self-imposed boundaries.

I am enormously grateful for the work of my coauthor, Brenda

Lane Richardson, who exemplifies the change financial literacy can bring to our lives, and to Ron King, Jr., for reading our manuscript and sharing his financial expertise. Our agent, Regina Brooks of Serendipity Literary Agency, has impressed me with her wide array of professional relationships and skill sets and helped us find the right publisher. Editors Christina Morgan and Dawn Davis provided much-appreciated advice.

Thanks also to Tena Krouse, owner of Y Not Now, in Richmond, Virginia, who developed our website Intheblackretirement .com. Attorney Melanie Lee offered advice on legacy and estate planning, and CPA Jim Holland was kind enough to answer some of my inquiries. Finally, I want to thank my tailor, George Clayton.

From Brenda Lane Richardson:

Thank you, God, for providing me with an opportunity to experience true freedom through financial planning. Thanks also to my immediate family: the Reverend Dr. W. Mark Richardson and our children, H. P. Worthington, Carolyn, and Mark junior.

I am grateful to Aaron and Pat Smith for their top-notch professionalism.

My hearty thanks to Mary Beth Franklin of *Kiplinger's Personal Finance* for endorsing this book, to Denise Williams, for her unerring editor's eye, and to Regina Brooks, agent extraordinaire. Thanks also to Christina Morgan and Dawn Davis of HarperCollins.

Valerie Coleman Morris supported this project from its inception and graciously shared her story. Glinda Bridgforth generously recommended me to Aaron Smith as a coauthor for this work, and E. Percil Stanford, Ph.D., chief diversity officer of AARP, offered much-needed encouragement at the book's inception. Gerald Harris, the founder of Harris Planning and Strategy Consulting in San

Francisco, real estate broker Nancy Lehrkind of the Grubb Company in Piedmont, California, and the Reverend Dr. Mark A. Croston, Sr., of the East End Baptist Church in Suffolk, Virginia, shared their seasoned expertise. Finally, thank you, Shirley Tarlton, for your warm greetings, and Sonja Tucker, an A. W. Smith financial adviser, for taking my last-minute questions.

Introduction

How Reading This Book
Can Change Your Financial Future

Early one morning, Dr. Evelyn Greene entered my office in Richmond, Virginia. The sturdily built, mahogany-toned woman of sixty-one wore a close-cropped salt-and-pepper natural and an elegant red suit. A church deacon had phoned the night before urging me to see Dr. Greene on an emergency basis to discuss the loss of her retirement savings fund.

I've helped clients with any number of money issues. In recent years my practice has increasingly focused on retirement planning. With an estimated 9 million black baby boomers preparing to leave the workforce, many are panicking about not having enough money to live on for the rest of their lives. Thanks be to God, the message is starting to get around that it's not too late to prepare for retirement.

That's probably true for you, too. If you've delayed retirement planning because you think you won't have enough money to last the rest of your life, *In the Black* can help. You'll learn to handle money in much the same way our mothers and grandmothers dealt with food—by taking what they had and stretching it till there was enough.

If you're consumed with worry and have been mentally beating yourself up for procrastinating, *In the Black* can help. This nine-step action plan offers a cure for retirement paralysis and proven methods for catching up. If you think you don't have a head for numbers and financial terms, take heart. *In the Black* will help you create a game plan you can follow as you develop financial literacy. When it comes to understanding how retirement planning works, whether you're at the kindergarten stage or the graduate-school level, *In the Black*'s step-by-step guide will help you get where you need to go. And if you thought that retirement planning was just for the wealthy, you're about to learn otherwise.

The nine action steps are designed to help you develop long-term strategies to secure your financial future, from figuring out how much you'll need during retirement to keeping money flowing to meet future expenses. There is no unified retirement plan in the United States, so folks often wind up pulling together scraps—like our elders making quilts: a few odds and ends from this tax-deferred plan, bits and pieces of government and employee benefits, and whatever our individual efforts have managed to yield. This catch-as-catch-can approach is fine for a quilting bee, but not for our survival in the future.

The key is planning, and even a small bit makes a difference. Researchers found that people who did a significant amount of retirement preparation had a median net worth of $200,000, compared with $84,000 for those who did the least. Even those who did only a little planning were ahead, with a median net worth of $172,000.

Planning pays off because it's a crucial psychological trigger. The results of an Ariel/Schwab 2006 Black Investors Survey found that African American workers who got help from financial advisers contributed more on a monthly basis to their retirement plans than those who didn't. And I can tell you from my own personal experience that we are far more likely to respond to advice that's tailored to our sensibilities and culture.

Working through this book, you'll get to know African Americans grappling with retirement issues who hail from throughout the United States. Over the years, A. W. Smith Financial Group* has developed a diverse pool of clients, launched a website, and conducted seminars with organizations that range from the American Business Women's Association to church investment groups. I started out by working with people in my home base of Richmond, Virginia, a city with a small-town feel despite being the state capital, with three universities and more than 194,000 residents, 57 percent of them black.

As the *Richmond Times-Dispatch* once pointed out, what distinguishes A. W. Smith from other financial firms in the area is that I started my practice working with people I knew from local black churches. Many of these clients know both me and Pat, my wife of seventeen years. This is the woman who, in daily acts of love and devotion, oversees our growing staff and keeps our business running efficiently. Our early clients came to us because they knew someone who knew us through our involvement in two Baptist churches, North Gayton and Quioccasin, which I have attended all of my forty-three years. A new client learned about our practice recently through our children, fourteen-year-old Jasmine and ten-year-old Aaron Justin, who participate in a church youth group. In that respect, we're growing into a full family business.

---

*A. W. Smith Financial Group, Inc., offers securities and advisory services through Centaurus Financial, Inc., a registered broker/dealer, member FINRA/SIPC.

Today our staff of financial advisers offers comprehensive planning for more than seven hundred individuals in various states. We also serve corporations and lead workshops and seminars. In addition to focusing on retirement planning, we help clients who want to finance mortgages, purchase insurance, and invest in stocks, bonds, and mutual funds.

This book is written to help improve your financial literacy, so that you can make informed choices and become ever more capable in managing your money, particularly as you look down the road toward retirement. More than 37 million Americans are over sixty-five, and 30 million more will reach that age by 2018. The media bombards consumers with messages about the need to plan for retirement. But are folks really paying attention?

One study found that most people nearing retirement are likely to ignore commercials that warn of financial catastrophe if they don't start saving more.

It's not surprising that people don't trust commerical messages, but who *are* they willing to listen to? A Nielsen survey found that most consumers look to loved ones, coworkers, friends, and neighbors as their most trusted sources of information when trying to decide which products and services to buy. That's right: In an age when messages can be sent around the world at the click of a computer key, word of mouth is the most trusted selling tool.

The church deacon who had phoned me about Dr. Greene hadn't offered many details about her crisis. He had told me about her background, explaining that fifteen years earlier Dr. Greene had quit her job as a secretary and with money from the sale of her house had completed an undergraduate degree, then earned a master's and Ph.D. in French before working her way up to cochair at a university linguistics department.

Right off the bat, it was easy to see how she had accomplished so much in midlife. With a take-charge attitude and brisk gestures,

Dr. Greene began pulling financial documents from a snakeskin attaché, offering brief explanations. When I asked how I might be of help, she began to fight off tears.

"I don't know where else to turn," she said. "The company that employed me as a secretary for twenty-five years provided a pension and also paid fifteen percent of my salary annually into a retirement savings account. I went back to college knowing that if things didn't work out, at least in my old age I could rely on Social Security and pension payments, along with my retirement account, which grew to two hundred thousand dollars." In a whisper, she added, "That account is empty now. I owe the government more than forty-five thousand dollars, and they're threatening to garnish my salary. A lawyer says the IRS could put liens on my Social Security and pension." She bent her head and covered her eyes, hiding her tears.

I assured her that I would help her make the right decisions so she could move forward in what had already been a remarkable life. She pointed to a lease agreement for a storefront building and spoke in a monotone, as if to keep her feelings at bay. "I loaned eighty thousand dollars to a friend to start a bookstore. He never repaid me and lied for months about paying rent, so I owe that, too. I won't get the deposit back either. He didn't clean the place before he took off."

Our conversation ended when a secretary buzzed to alert me that my first scheduled client of the day had arrived. Dr. Greene and I agreed to meet again in a week, to give me time to examine her documents and devise a strategy. She left with downcast eyes, her shoulders slumped.

Her story might seem extreme, but it's hardly unique. We don't often hear about retirement debacles, because people caught in desperate straits are often so ashamed that they tend to be secretive about their mistakes. Through the years, I've heard countless stories from clients about acquaintances or loved ones suffering terrible setbacks after making poor financial decisions.

My early experience as a credit analyst, when I helped those maxed out on debt, heightened my sensitivity to the shame people feel about the inevitable results of poor money-management skills. Dr. Greene was a proud woman and obviously embarrassed about sharing details of her private life. But she needn't have worried on that score.

I'm mindful of guarding my clients' privacy. To that end, I've changed the names and all the identifiable biographical details of the clients discussed in this book. In years of working as a financial counselor, I've also made it a point not to be judgmental. How could I be? A dentist doesn't judge a patient for not having perfect teeth. In fact, that dentist might feel gratitude at being allowed to repair the damage. Similarly, others with specialized skills, from carpenters to surgeons, wouldn't look down on clients for not having their expertise. Most likely they would be grateful, just as I am for this opportunity to help you learn how to thrive when you retire.

Financial literacy isn't something most people learn at home. My dad, Johnnie Smith, now seventy years old, drove a truck, and my mother, Louise Smith, sixty, worked as a domestic. God bless them both. Even if they had understood the intricacies of finance, they were too caught up in the day-to-day struggle of keeping a roof over our heads to think about teaching my brother and me how to manage money.

Perhaps, like me, you didn't grow up watching your parents plan for retirement. Financial planning wasn't taught in school either. Regardless of statistics you may have read about African Americans lagging behind white people in retirement planning, my experience of working with clients of all races suggests that most people had experiences that weren't very different from mine and are now trying to make up for lost time, desperate to learn how to break through years of lethargy in planning for retirement.

Still, a lot of highly educated people like Dr. Greene get angry with themselves about poor monetary decisions. They figure they should have known better. It's not a matter of intelligence though, but of knowledge. Financial literacy is empowering, and not just mentally. It translates into a heftier bottom line.

In a study in which people were quizzed on simple calculations, such as compound interest or percentages, their knowledge was compared with their net worth. Researchers found that more correct answers matched up with greater wealth. Those who grasped a subject like compound interest had a median net worth of $309,000, versus $116,000 for those who didn't know the answers. That difference of $193,000 helps explain why financial literacy is critical. To that end, you'll notice key financial terms and phrases reviewed in easy-to-find financial literacy building blocks.

> **FINANCIAL LITERACY:**
> The ability to make informed financial choices and analyze money matters

Financial literacy is more than simply knowing the right words; it's a way of being. Financially literate people get the most out of their money, including sustained growth. They would be just as likely to read *Kiplinger's*, *Black Enterprise*, or *Money* magazine as they would a fashion or sports publication. Financially literate people get so excited about the positive changes they've made in their lives that they strive to learn more, listening, for instance, to CDs by money guru Suze Orman or attending financial empowerment seminars.

You may already know that the term *in the black* means "profit-able," as opposed to *in the red*, which means "losing money." We have come a long way as a people, and make no mistake about it, there is money in our community. Black American economic buy-ing power in 2002 was $646 billion, a figure that climbed to $800 billion in 2007. And the saying, "You ain't seen nothin' yet" cer-tainly applies to our future. By 2012, black buying power is expected to reach $1.1 trillion, according to the Nielsen Company.

My coauthor, Brenda Lane Richardson, and I titled our book *In the Black* as a statement of who we are as a people with roots in the African Diaspora; in recognition of the growth we've experi-enced collectively; and to challenge you, the reader, to transform your financial life into a reflection of all that you are and all that you can be.

The client stories woven throughout the book are written to shed insight into problems that you might be grappling with. Some of these individuals have been impacted by the income disparity and credit discrimination that impedes financial security for many African Americans. But many individuals we've included counter prevailing stereotypes of us as socially and economically marginal. Far from homogenous, my client list represents the socioeconomic spectrum. Bonnie, fifty-nine, a newspaper executive and the wife of an IBM manager, plans to start her own luxury-goods business when she retires. Renee, thirty-six, a science teacher and single parent, has gone into debt paying her son's college tuition and sup-porting her elderly infirm father—all the while saving for her own retirement so she won't also wind up destitute. Jamal, forty-two, a security guard, seldom spends time with his wife, Kinesha, a hotel domestic. They've staggered their schedules to take turns caring for their toddlers.

There is plenty that folks like Bonnie, Renee, Jamal, and Kine-sha do *not* have in common. What they do have in common is the need for a plan to help them remain financially secure after retirement, and that is the basis for this book.

When Dr. Greene returned to my office a week later, I'd come up with ideas to help her regain her footing. I asked about the "financial adviser" she consulted before meeting me. She said he worked at the bank where she kept her checking account.

Let me say that such titles as "financial adviser," "financial counselor," "retirement planner," and any number of variants have little meaning. What's important is that you find a financial professional whom you can trust to address your particular needs and possibilities. I'm a *personal* registered financial consultant. Although I don't use the word *personal* as a professional designation, I stress it here to convey that I work with clients over a period of weeks to gather information, listening to them, even taping their conversations so I can later review what they've said. I try to understand what's important to clients. I want them to know that I'm serious about helping them find a way to live comfortably. I offer advice that I believe to be in their best interests. I hope that working through this book will help you solidify your retirement plans, regardless of whether you work independently or with a professional.

Some financial advisers are essentially salespeople who want to push certain products or convince clients to make unwise investments. I'll tell you more about how to find a financial adviser who works to meet your needs in step 8 in chapter eighteen. In Dr. Greene's case, before she moved her nest egg, the adviser at her bank steered her in the right direction, recommending that she "directly roll over" the $200,000 from her retirement savings account into an IRA. Although these terms will be defined later in this book, let me offer a brief explanation.

Dr. Greene's savings were in a *401(k)*. Named for a section of the Internal Revenue Code, this is an employer-sponsored retirement savings plan. A plan similar to a 401(k) but offered to employees of nonprofit organizations, schools, and hospitals is a 403(b). Similarly, public employees might receive a 457 retirement plan. Federal employees have the Thrift Savings Plan (TSP), while small-business owners can set up Keoghs (pronounced "key-ohs") and solo(k)s are available for one-person businesses. There are variations in the ways in which these tax-deferred retirement vehicles operate. Sometimes the money is deducted from salary; sometimes an employer is the sole contributor or matches what the employee is contributing. What these plans have in common is that they allow invested, tax-deferred funds to accumulate until they are withdrawn, once the account holder reaches a certain age.

For now, let's focus on Dr. Greene's story. The money in her 401(k) accrued year after year as her employer deposited money into her account. At one point a financial adviser at her bank recommended that Dr. Greene move the money into an IRA, to make it more tax efficient for her heirs at the time of her death.

The IRA, or individual retirement account, allows individuals to save money tax-free for retirement independently.

The financial adviser at the bank told Dr. Greene that she should transfer the 401(k) money to an IRA in a direct rollover, a transfer of funds in which money is rolled like a ball directly from one retirement account to another. When I work with clients, I oversee these transactions to ensure that no mistakes are made, because errors can be costly. The problem occurred when the bank's financial adviser didn't follow up to make certain that the transfer went smoothly—and because Dr. Greene wasn't financially literate. She struck out on her own without understanding the rules governing retirement vehicles. Here's how her savings dwindled to nothing:

1. She asked the company that was holding her 401(k) money to send her a check payable to her. If she had told the com-

pany to send the money directly to ABC Company (where she was purchasing her IRA), or if she had asked that the check be made payable to the ABC Company, for the benefit of Dr. Greene, then her savings would have remained intact. Instead, because the check was issued in her name, the company's administrative department, as required by law, withheld $24\frac{1}{2}$ percent off the top (a 10 percent penalty for premature distribution, since she was not yet fifty-nine and a half, plus 10 percent for the federal government as an advance on the taxes, and another $4\frac{1}{2}$ percent in state taxes. State taxes vary from state to state.). In a case such as this, the goverment overwithholds to protect itself from having to hire a revenue agent to go after the taxpayer for large tax bills. In the end, Dr. Greene was charged $49,000 in taxes and penalties and overwithholding. *Her account balance was down to $151,000.*

2. Dr. Greene deposited her remaining money into the IRA within sixty days, as required for a rollover. She had her bank send the ABC Company a check for $151,000. What she didn't know was that a critical rule governing rollovers required her to put the same amount in her IRA as had been in her 401(k)—$200,000.

3. That spring, Dr. Greene received a huge tax bill. The federal and state governments viewed her as having withdrawn her retirement savings prematurely and thus considered it income. As far as the government was concerned, her income included $200,000 plus her salary from the university. She doled out an extra $60,000 in taxes, which she withdrew from her remaining $151,000 retirement account. *Her balance was down to $91,000.*

4. A year later she withdrew $80,000 from the IRA to help her friend start a bookstore, and she was again penalized for premature distribution at a 10 percent penalty, and 4½ percent for the state government. She was down another $91,600. By then her retirement account was wiped out, and she paid $600 out of pocket. *Her retirement balance was zero.*

5. Again, at tax time, her premature withdrawal of $80,000 was treated as income, along with her salary. *Her tax bill was $46,400.*

That's when I met her. With $25,000 due for the rent on the store and a $46,400 tax bill, Dr. Greene was $71,000 in the red.

Here's what happened next. We arranged for an auctioneer to sell the books so the store could be cleared out, and Dr. Greene recouped her $5,000 rental deposit on the store. The sale of the books brought in $50,000, which was deposited in a high-interest savings account.

Then we went up against the big guys. We visited the company that had held her 401(k). A lot of people are unaware of this, but often company policies require employees to tape their conversations with account holders. I asked them to pull Dr. Greene's tape on the date she made a request for withdrawal, and we listened to it. We spent a tense few minutes when the tape started, but as we heard Dr. Greene's cultured tones, we both heaved a sigh of relief. Dr. Greene had asked for a direct rollover. The company was at fault for not making the rollover direct.

We asked the company to go back and correct its mistake, and it did. We sent the IRS a copy of the tape, along with the company's admission of error. The IRS agreed to repair the damage, and

Dr. Greene was only penalized on the $80,000 premature with-drawal. At this point she'd paid out so much in taxes that the IRS owed her a refund. A year later, her savings was restored to $150,000, and the IRS was off her back.

Best of all, Dr. Greene continued talking with me, discussing her hopes and dreams for retirement and analyzing what she would need and how to catch up. If she remains on track, she will be able to fund her dreams. She has sent several of her academic colleagues my way, and she's a major proponent of financial literacy. Having learned from her mistakes, she wants to keep others from following in her footsteps.

These days when I see her, she looks luminescent. She has moved on to a new life, one that's in the black. She is one of several clients you'll hear about in this book who transformed their financial lives.

In preparation for your work, please make room in a file for financial documents you will need to collect and organize as we proceed, and purchase a notebook to use as a journal.

We are about to embark on a spiritual journey. You can begin by imagining that I am right beside you, but not in front. The Lord is always in the lead. To that end, each of the twenty chapters is followed by a scriptural passage, so you can begin your next chapter with the kind of energy that faith can inspire. The New Revised Standard Version is used for all scriptural quotations. This work was written to address African Americans in a Christian context, but one need not be of a particular religion or race to benefit from it.

"Listen to advice and accept instruction, that you may gain wisdom for the future." —Proverbs 19:20.

If the spirit moves you, read this passage aloud and write about its meaning as you become more financially literate.

_____

_____

_____

_____

_____

_____

_____

_____

_____

STEP 1

Figure Out What You Really Want

1

Defining Your Values

I'd met Lee Ann Haines earlier, but I was meeting her husband for the first time when they arrived at my office. At fifty-seven, Roosevelt Haines still towered over people; I later learned that he grew up playing basketball in Harlem. After fighting in Vietnam, he was recruited by the Chapel Hill Police Department, in North Carolina, where he worked as a detective. Mrs. Haines, fifty-nine, a pleasantly round woman, was a cook for an elementary school cafeteria. She boasted of being a native North Carolinian.

Months earlier, when I led a retirement seminar for county employees, Mrs. Haines had introduced herself. She told me that I was the person she'd been looking for. Now she was giving me a kind smile, in stark contrast to her husband's scowl. I wasn't offended by his wariness. A police detective would often be reminded in his work of the human propensity to do wrong. His demeanor suggested that he felt his wife had dragged him in to talk to some guy who either would try to convince him to buy something they didn't need or might lose or steal their hard-earned savings.

Mr. Haines questioned me thoroughly about my background and relaxed somewhat when he learned that, in addition to being a registered financial consultant, I was qualified as a fiduciary adviser. This designation requires a minimum of five years' experience, passing a rigorous background check and exam, and a thorough analysis of hundreds of clients, all of whom are asked to rate the adviser's work and skill level.

Mr. Haines didn't know me, but I wasn't working at the same disadvantage. He and his wife had filled out a questionnaire asking, among other things, marital status (they'd been married fifteen years) and whether they had any children (he had three adult children from his first marriage and two school-aged grandchildren). I'd also learned from their forms that they loved Italian food, and that he enjoyed reading military-history books and listening to jazz, while she loved the best-selling *Chicken Soup for the Soul* series and African American–themed novels.

I asked what I consider an essential question for retirement planning: "What is most important to each of you?"

Mrs. Haines was about to answer when her husband heaved an impatient sigh. "What has this got to do with our retirement?"

It was an excellent question, and you may be wondering the same thing. At least one out of ten clients respond this way when I ask them what they value. They might assume that I'm trying to soften them up before I make a sales pitch, or they see it as a time waster. Like the Cuba Gooding character in the film *Jerry Maguire*, I get the sense that they want to shout, "Show me the money." And in the event you're also thinking of skipping this phase of the work so you can rush to the bottom line, you should know that that would be akin to constructing a house without laying the foundation.

You can find retirement advisers who will skip this part of the process. In fact, you can open an account online and fill in the blanks on a form, or phone the company and someone will ask you for bare-bones details before suggesting a plan. The idea is to sell you a product so they can get on to the next client. It's about speed, like heating a mug of soup mix in a microwave. While it might satisfy you temporarily, it's nothing like having a bowl of rich broth and oxtails, like what my grandma Chips often had simmering on her stove.

Instant retirement-planning conversations are seldom helpful in the long run, because no real connection is made. In seeking to connect, I ask clients about everything from favorite books and food preferences because I can't give them information that will help them make independent and sound decisions to accomplish their financial goals if I don't know them. As a matter of fact, I'd turn away an individual who refused to go through this process or if I became convinced that this person's only goal was to build wealth quickly and take lots of risks.

Maybe you're thinking that you don't need to go through this process because you already know yourself. But no matter how well you know yourself, this work is designed to increase your self-awareness. It has been tested over time, and it works.

Before long, Mr. Haines was saying that most of all he valued family. Minutes later, his wife's mouth fell open as he admitted why he'd resisted planning for retirement, even though it had probably meant missing out on financial opportunities.

He said that years before, his first girlfriend had gotten pregnant, and her parents had sent her to Ohio. If that child was alive, he said, he wanted to arrange a meeting. He added that he realized he hadn't wanted his money tied up in retirement savings just in case this son or daughter needed his financial help. His wife was clearly irritated about being kept in the dark all these years. She'd never heard about this long-ago pregnancy, but she added that it was important to do the right thing. Reflecting on his values seemed to change Mr. Haines's attitude about planning for the future. He unclenched his hands, and his shoulders began to relax.

Now it's your turn to consider what's most important to you. Don't be surprised if the question makes you feel a little anxious. Planning for the future can heighten anxiety. Some years back, Allstate Insurance asked people about their greatest concerns. While reading their responses, consider whether you've had similar fears.

- Ability to pay bills in case of a disability (81 percent)
- Fear their money won't last (77 percent)
- Ability to pay for children's education (77 percent)
- Ability to afford health care (63 percent)
- Family's lifestyle changes in case of death (62 percent)
- Financially unsure about retirement (62 percent)
- Ability to replace cars in case of an accident (62 percent)
- Worry about becoming homeless (42 percent)
- Getting Alzheimer's (35 percent)

In the box on the next page, record any of your own concerns and tie them to what matters most to you. Use a pencil in this and upcoming exercises so you can make changes easily.

I am concerned about . . .	So what's important to me is . . .
Example: My daughter is struggling as a single parent with two kids	providing for my grandchildren to attend college

Another approach for focusing on your values involves the next simple exercise. In the left-hand column, list the tangibles (things you can see, hear, touch, or smell) that you once believed or still believe will make you happy, such as a new car. When Pat and I first composed our list, we certainly included buying our own home.

Tangibles That Matter to Me	Intangibles That Matter to Me
1. Example: house	1. Example: financial security
2.	2.
3.	3.
4.	4.
5.	5.

When you've finished writing in both columns, circle the tangibles and intangibles that continue to be of enduring significance. Try to quell any self-criticism. For instance, it doesn't make you a good or bad person if you circled something such as "jewelry." Maybe what you're saying is that it's important to you to look successful. If you circled "new home," perhaps you're saying that you value financial independence. A lot of people find that what they most value is love, faith, financial independence, stress-free living, and good health.

At this point it might help if I contextualize the word *value*. Originally it was strictly an economic term to help measure the worth of something. Even today, when goods are bought and sold, the value is determined by how much people are willing to pay for them, and that's key here. Our values guide our financial actions. For instance, if we value family, one way to demonstrate that is by helping provide for the needs of family members. Economic language has given the word *value* a larger meaning. Values are the beliefs in which we have emotional investments, the standards and principles that guide our financial actions. That's why, before we plan our financial future, we have to understand our values.

With that in mind, look back over the lists of what you once considered important but did not circle. Maybe you wrote "partying," which suggests that you valued living for the moment. Whatever it was, you'll probably find that over the course of your lifetime, you've spent a lot of money to support those values. Maybe your values have shifted, or maybe not. Either way, understanding them is an important first step in what can actually be a joyful and fulfilling process of retirement planning.

It might seem odd that a financial adviser is writing about joy and fulfillment, but there's nothing new about tying emotions to money. Mr. Haines, for instance, felt a mix of relief and disappointment after he located his first girlfriend and learned that her pregnancy had just been a rumor. In recognizing his longing for this phantom child, he was able to put love of family into perspective. From that point he made it clear that before he left this earth he wanted to create a financial legacy for his children.

In addition to wanting financial comfort, his wife listed her desire to spend more time volunteering, to increase her offerings to her church, and to have peace of mind. Like the Haineses, you will discover that retirement planning isn't only about money. That's what trips up so many people. Retirement planning is about your present life and your future. It's not about the number of things or dollars that you have; it's about relationships and happiness.

For a minute, I'll imagine that you're sitting on the other side of my desk and that I have an idea about what will make you happy. Like all of us, you have a need for joy and a sense of belonging. What you'll learn in this work is how to connect those needs to money. Everybody wants to feel happy. If happiness could be sold, it would fly off the shelves. But of course you can't buy it. If you doubt that, look at celebrity magazines. Some of the richest people are unhappy. Many of them get so caught up with material objects that their lives become disconnected from their values.

I'm reminded of that when I work as a financial adviser with the National Football League Players Association. The lives of these young athletes might sound glamorous, but the truth is, they're about twenty-two when they're shipped off to what may be unfamiliar cities. They're earning lots of money, but at the end of the day they're sitting in front of the television feeling sad and lonely.

I only played football in college, but I think back to summers at the University of Richmond, when my teammates and I suffered through fiercely hot days of practice: 7 A.M. until 10; then 2 P.M. until 4 o'clock; then back on the field again at 7 P.M., and later, another hour of studying our plays on film. I didn't have a girlfriend at the time, and although I did have buddies on the team, I got lonely. When I returned to the dorm at night, the first thing I always did was call my mama. Even if I'd had all the money in the world, I still would have wanted to talk to her and feel connected.

That's how I know that if I didn't encourage you to consider what makes you happy, I'd fail at helping you make the right decisions with your money. There's research to support my belief that happiness should be considered in retirement planning.

According to a report in the April 2007 issue of *The American Journal of Psychiatry*, a study of men who had unhappy childhoods or difficult middle years found that wealth had little to do with contentment during their retirement. What did? These men discovered that intangibles brought them the happiness that eluded them earlier in life. Among experiences that gave their lives a sense of purpose, they listed relationships and volunteering to help the less fortunate.

The results of some medical studies suggest that contentment-inducing activities such as improving relationships and volunteering can lead to a longer, healthier life, helping people who struggle with asthma, cardiovascular disease, weight loss, and insomnia and boosting the immune system in HIV patients.

Now I want you to prioritize your values. The fact that you even have the luxury of considering your values suggests that you are already blessed. Ask yourself what's most important to keep you going and place a "1" beside that value. Place a "2" beside whatever value comes next in importance and so on. When you've finished, save that list for the next chapter, in which I'll explain how values can translate into long-range goals.

MY VALUES

_____

_____

_____

_____

_____

_____

If you're in a committed relationship, consider inviting your partner to join you in this work. If you're single, invite a close relative, friend, or an entire group to join you in formulating your individual plans. If you teach at an adult Sunday school, consider leading congregants through this work.

> **INFLATION:**
> The upward movement of the prices of goods and services

BUILDING FINANCIAL LITERACY

Most of us have heard the word *inflation*. It refers to the continuing rise in prices. Part of the pleasure of watching movies and TV shows set in the past is imagining what we might have purchased at lower prices that would be worth lots more today. Try subtracting twenty years from your age, recalling what you paid for rent at that time or what houses and cars cost. Those prices are hard to believe, compared with today's prices. Of course, in our work we're looking toward the future, when prices—which reflect consumer demand, transportation, manufacturing costs, taxes, et cetera—will continue to rise.

Stories in the media paint terrifying images of how inflation will impact you when you're on a fixed income. For example, if your aunt set up a lifetime gift for you of $500 a month, that might cover the cost of your groceries and transportation today. Ten years from now, however, that same $500 might only cover the cost of your groceries. The thought of inflation might set off alarm bells in your head when it comes to planning for retirement. It might help to know that as you read this book, you will learn how to estimate what you'll need for your future and how to work your money so that for the rest of your life you'll remain in the black.

CONSIDERING SCRIPTURE

"Likewise all to whom God gives wealth and possessions and whom He enables to enjoy them, and to accept their lot and find enjoyment in their toil—this is the gift of God." —Ecclesiastes 5:19.
If the spirit moves you, read this passage aloud and write about its meaning as you become more financially literate.

2

Getting Your Goals Straight

Ordinarily we don't call clients by their first names in my practice. If folks insist otherwise, we add "Mrs." or "Miss" or 'Mr."—as in "Miss Mary" or "Mr. Larry." Some might view this as old-fashioned, but I believe in paying attention to the past as well as the future. The truth is that in our history, racists tried to demean us by ignoring our surnames and titles. So today, when my staff and I greet the men and women for whom we work, we use titles as grace notes of respectability.

There's always an exception, as with one hairstylist in my neck of the woods who likes to be called by one name: Silver. When she steps from her silver Benz wearing a sable coat, Silver looks like a celebrity. In fact, she attributes her success in an oversaturated field to her dramatic appearance.

The day I visited her silver-and-pink-veneered beauty salon, located within easy driving distance of Washington, D.C., and her high-profile clients, the thirty-four-year-old proprietress led me past several women getting new hairdos, pedicures, and manicures, and she pointed out that there were more customers in the massage and waxing rooms. Silver was understandably proud of what she'd created. I'd already learned that when she was nineteen and pregnant, her strict parents threw her out of their house. On her own, she raised her son while building her business, and when her sister-in-law later took to drugs and the streets, Silver invited her brother and two of his children to share her home. Savvy about money in many regards, she had long saved for her son's education. At fourteen he was earning straight As and aiming for an Ivy League college.

Silver settled behind her kidney-shaped chrome desk, remaining quiet until the door closed behind the assistant who'd served us steaming cups of cappuccino. Then she spoke in a rush. "I wanted you to see my shop because it's a part of me. When you asked me about goals, I started feeling guilty, although I don't know why. Almost every day for fifteen years, I've worked from the moment I woke up until I went to bed." She expelled a lungful of air. "When my son goes away to college in four years, I want to take time off from work and spend a year traveling around the world. I think I deserve it."

I couldn't have agreed more. But she hadn't hired me because she wanted permission to spend her own money. She wanted help in figuring out how to reach her goals without destroying what she'd created, and she stressed that she didn't want to imperil the funds she had put aside for a comfortable early retirement at age fifty.

In the previous chapter we considered values, cherished beliefs about what we want in our lives. In this second step of retirement planning, we explore value-directed goals, which are driven by spiritual, emotional, financial, and physical needs. Like markers on a road, value-directed goals can guide your actions and decisions and remind you that you're making progress. Up to this point, you may have drifted from one situation to the next without a clear plan. Now you're headed in the right direction.

Reaching a value-directed goal can energize you and help you eventually achieve more than you'd hoped for. Value-directed goals aren't ideas that just pop up into your head. They represent integral aspects of who you are, so before recording them, you'll want to make sure they meet certain criteria. For our purposes they should be specific, positive, realistic, beneficial to you, and measurable (which means you can tell whether you've made progress toward the goal, reached it, or surpassed it). Identifying goals will guide your activities and behaviors. I learned this from personal experiences.

I was seven when my parents moved our family from a rural neighborhood to inner-city Richmond, and the relocation turned out to be a culturally shocking ordeal. Although I learned quickly to defend myself, I was terrified and developed a stutter, which was humiliating. Kids made fun of me, and my new teachers assumed I was slow-witted. That was when I set my first conscious goal of learning to speak clearly.

I offered to do little chores for pay and saved until I could afford a tape player and a motivational tape. This was the early seventies, when you couldn't find tapes by African American speakers, like Les Brown. I listened to Zig Ziglar, a white man from Alabama and Mississippi.

I can still see myself as a seven-year-old, standing in the mirror mimicking him: "You were born to win. But to be a winner, you must plan to win, prepare to win, and expect to win." It wasn't just my speech that improved; these exercises bolstered my determination to succeed. It took years of practice, but as my stuttering eased, I grew more ambitious. Still shy, I joined the church choir to get accustomed to standing in front of people. And in high school I joined a student political organization and learned to speak persuasively. Today I earn my living by communicating with others. I was able to reach my goal of improving my speech because it was in keeping with who I am, and it helped to convince me that I could improve my life.

Figuring out your financial goals can improve your life. A joint study by the University of Pennsylvania and Dartmouth College found that people with financial goals have twice the wealth of people who have only vague ideas about what they want.

Silver's goal to travel tapped into a core belief. Education topped her list of values. When I asked her to translate that into a positive action, she identified two goals: educating her son and herself. She wasn't interested in returning to school. After spending most of her adult life within the confines of her salon, she was eager to see the world, rather than just hear about it from globe-trotting clients. She already looked sophisticated; she hoped that learning about other cultures would help her feel that way.

I'm sharing her story because it underscores the significance of value-directed goals in retirement planning and the benefits of financial strategizing for everyone, whether rich or struggling. Silver was ready to move forward.

Here's how we proceeded. She formulated her goals, just as you can by looking over your prioritized list of values and choosing the top five. I encourage clients to make sure their own interests are represented at or near the top of this list. Ask yourself what you care about when it comes to providing for yourself. Some people are so selfless that they forget their own needs. Please don't put yourself last; this is your future that you're considering. In the boxes that follow, pencil in your values, starting with what you consider most important.

Under "Value" Silver wrote, "Education." Whatever your answer, describe how you would demonstrate the importance of this

VALUE-DIRECTED GOAL CHART

VALUE	ACTION/ IMPORTANCE	VALUE-DIRECTED GOAL	TARGET DATE	ESTIMATED COST

quality in your life. In other words, what do you want to do about it? Write your answer under "Action/Importance" by starting with a verb. (Silver wrote, "Give my son the best education possible.") Then narrow your answer down to something specific, focusing on what you have the capacity to accomplish. I asked Silver what it meant to her to give her son the best education. She wrote: "Pay for him to attend college and graduate school." This action was her first value-directed goal.

What are your value-directed goals? A lot of people tell me they value independence, but sometimes the way they state that is "I don't ever want to depend on anyone for help." When I ask them to state that in a positive way, they might write, "Maintain my good health." I encourage them—as I encourage you—to keep boiling answers down and translate them into actions. A person who wants to maintain good health might write, "Get health insurance."

Wherever you are in this process, don't stop at your first or second answer. Continue searching for specific goals you would like to achieve. If you want to maintain your independence, one of your value-directed goals might be "Paying off my mortgage" or "Saving enough money to last my lifetime."

After you have figured out your most important goal, write down a target date for accomplishing it. Include the year, month, and day. A specific date will make you feel more accountable.

For now, you'll only need to estimate the costs of each goal. But you can make informed guesses by asking yourself specific questions, such as whether you want your child to attend college in state or out of state. Private or public college? Whatever goal you select, estimate its cost.

As Silver and I continued through this process, we found that she would need another $100,000 over what she'd already saved to send her son to a private college and graduate school. For goal two, traveling, we came up with a $90,000 figure. For goal three, taking off a year from work, we estimated that she would lose about $100,000 in business revenues, so we added that amount to her costs. For goal four, retiring at fifty and maintaining her standard of living, she planned to pump $25,000 annually for fourteen years, a total of $350,000, into a Simplified Employment Pension IRA, a 401(k)-type plan designed for self-employed and small business owners. Her final goal, to continue supplementing her seventy-three-year-old mother's pension, at the cost of $20,000 annually, came to an estimated $360,000. Silver's total came to $1 million.

In my business we ask clients, "What is your price?" Silver's "price" was $1 million. Putting a dollar figure to retirement goals makes sense in financial planning. You probably wouldn't buy shoes, a car, or even a pizza without asking about the cost. Why should your retirement be any different? Here are some directions you can follow.

DETERMINING YOUR PRICE

1. For the time being, without factoring for inflation or taxes, estimate your current annual overhead, which means how much it costs you each year to keep going. Write that sum on the line provided on the next page.

2. If you haven't already, determine when you want to retire. Pencil in a month, day, and year. What age will you be? Include that information.

3. Next you can estimate how much you'll need after you retire. According to the National Center for Health, on the average, black men live to 69.2 years, while black women live to 76.1 years. Of course lots of people live into their eighties and beyond. Since no one but God knows how long you'll live, consider the ages of your parents and

grandparents when they died, and factor in your health. If you're just learning retirement planning, you'll want to keep things simple. So beneath the "overhead" figure, write down the age you imagine you will live to on the "longevity" line.

Overhead: _____

Longevity: _____

Retirement date: _____

Age at retirement: _____

Years in retirement ____ x Annual overhead ____ = My price: ____

4. Now calculate accordingly. For instance, at forty-two, you might plan to retire at the age of sixty-five. Let's assume that you will live to age eighty-seven, twenty-two years after retirement. At $30,000 a year for overhead, you would need $660,000. Here's how to estimate the costs for your needs: Multiply the number of years in retirement by the cost of your annual overhead. If that's one of your goals, add it to the Value-Directed Goal Chart on page 32. How about other goals? You can add those as well.

5. Calculate the total for all your goals, and then you'll know your price.

Determining one's price can provoke strong responses. It's natural to feel apprehensive; those numbers seem out of reach. This phase of retirement planning is like entering a haunted house, because you don't know what's going to pop up next. If you find that you're frightened, try taking a calming breath. And remember that you can only be hurt by what you don't know. Your continued participation is a trust issue. It's to your advantage to keep moving along with me. You don't want to be left in the dark.

Before moving on, ask yourself whether there are any goals you might want to add or eliminate. Or perhaps you'll want to scale down a goal or enlarge it. Be prepared for insights. The goal-making process helped Silver realize why she felt guilty about the prospect of taking her journey. She phoned to tell me she'd come to a major revelation about why she was feeling guilty.

"I earn a lot, and I could pull this off, but I realize that I have a sixth goal. My brother can afford to take care of his younger girls, who live with us, but I haven't told you about his two other daughters. They were raised by someone else and didn't have a mother or father to speak of. My brother had his troubles. He was an addict and he abandoned those girls. They're teenagers now, smart. I've had them come by the shop and help out, given them pocket money. But I've never really done anything for them. Now that I have something, I can't do to them what my mother did to me—tell them they're on their own. I want to invest in them. I've decided to spend the money I would have used for the trip and save it for their education. How else could they get to college?"

The sense of responsibility Silver felt for her mother and nieces is not unusual in my practice. Providing for extended-family members is a key value for many whose ancestors hail from the African Diaspora. Strong kinship ties explain why we often refer to friends or others who are not related by blood as "aunts" and "uncles."

These emotional bonds date back to African tribal culture and were reinforced during slavery when families were torn asunder, as sold-away parents relied on fellow captives to "look after my baby." The notion was bolstered during the Great Migration, when those African Americans who made it to the big cities sent money "down home" to help others. Support included educating siblings and extended-family members, and many in the North invited southern relatives to join them until they could get settled.

Kinship ties endure today. Michigan State University professor Dr. Harriet P. McAdoo credits the kinship system as a key factor in upward mobility for many African Americans. Kinship ties should be taken into account, especially as in relation to retirement planning for African Americans. According to a 2006 Ariel/Charles Schwab study of people with higher incomes, 27 percent of the African Americans polled had adults other than a spouse living in their homes, which is significantly higher than families of other races.

The study confirmed that many of us who are concerned about saving for our children's educations or caring for elderly parents are considerably less likely to be saving for retirement. That shouldn't be surprising. Just as college tuition is rising at a fast clip, so are the costs of caring for elderly parents. One study found that on average people pay about $5,500 annually to care for aging relatives or spouses, and that figure increases by $3,000 when we provide long-distance care.

Obviously not every black person feels the need to support family members. We're all individuals, and the notion of kinship isn't universally appreciated. "I have nine sisters and brothers, and none of them are as good as I am about saving, so they come to me for loans," groaned Kevin Brown, a tax attorney from Maryland and longtime client. "They think that since I'm single and don't have kids that *I'm the bank*." He laughed, explaining that he bought his mother a refrigerator and paid for her vacation recently, but that's his mom. For years he helped his siblings and friends with emergency loans, staving off their foreclosures, wage garnishings, and repossession crises. And he pointed out that he never charged interest, even on loans as large as $10,000. The debts were always repaid, but now, he emphasized, "the bank is closed."

Silver did feel responsible for her family though. With the

needs of others balanced on her shoulders, she was prepared to give up her dream of traveling. But did she have to? My next question dealt with who had custody of her teenage nieces. I asked whether they were in foster care.

She seemed embarrassed. "I had no choice. My brother wasn't doing well, and I didn't have any money back then. So yes, they're in foster care."

From a financial standpoint, their foster-care status proved to be a tremendous advantage. Silver's teenage nieces qualified for the Education and Training Vouchers (ETV) Program that was designed to assist foster children and adopted youth with college education and employment training. These vouchers can help pay for tuition, room and board, books, supplies, and transportation. The ETV Program is available in most states. For more information, go online to www.statevoucher.org.

I often get looks of stunned disbelief from clients when I give them this kind of information, and that was exactly what happened on this occasion. I don't think Silver could trust herself to believe me until after she'd researched it herself and confirmed it.

This occurred five years ago, before Silver's son was accepted at Yale and before she booked her travel tour. She sent me a card when she visited Senegal, writing that she was learning a lot about other cultures and even more about herself.

What have you realized about your goals? Give yourself time to consider these ideas. When you're ready to start pursuing goals, work on one at a time and break each one into listings of specific tasks. One client who wanted to sell her home and move to another state so she could live closer to her family worked in baby steps, making two to three calls a week at first and planning them into her schedule. Her workload grew heavier eventually, but the task-oriented approach kept her from feeling overwhelmed.

This kind of planning can transform views about time. Advertisers have convinced us that we have little of it, which is why we presumably need their time-saving products. In the next chapter, you will find that you do have sufficient time.

HELPFUL HINT

If you haven't already done so, please gather your financial documents and, if necessary, write to institutions or firms to get the needed paperwork. These documents might include payroll stubs; recent income-tax returns; mortgage paperwork; statements from Social Security, loan, and credit card companies, retirement savings, pension plans, checking and passbook savings accounts, CDs and money market accounts, and stock or bond investments.

Check off the documents you have collected on the following list:

- ❒ Payroll stubs
- ❒ Bank statements
- ❒ Income-tax returns
- ❒ Social Security statements
- ❒ Mortgage or lease agreement
- ❒ Loan and credit card statements
- ❒ Savings and checking accounts
- ❒ CDs
- ❒ Money market accounts
- ❒ (401)k-type retirement savings plans
- ❒ Stocks, bonds, and other investments
- ❒ Insurance policies
- ❒ Miscellaneous

For your receipts, use three separate folders with pockets marked "Tax Receipts" for big-ticket items and those that can be deducted; "Take-Action Receipts" for expense accounts, rebates, and proofs of mailing, et cetera; and "Temporary Receipts" for bank-deposit slips, et cetera.

BUILDING FINANCIAL LITERACY

Silver's savings grew because the interest *compounded*.

> **COMPOUNDING:**
> When interest is added to the principal, making the money increase exponentially, as returns add to returns

Here's how compounding works. Let's say you deposit $2,000 and earn $80 interest. The $2,080 is then redeposited, and the next year, you earn $83—a little bit more. The $2,163 is allowed to increase; then this is repeated. Gains continue to be realized on the original investment, and a greater return is realized on top of that, potentially year after year. Dee Lee and Jim Flewelling, authors of *The Complete Idiot's Guide to Retiring Early* (Alpha, 2001), describe compounding as the eighth wonder of the world, because "you earn a return on your initial investment, and then you earn a return on your return. . . . In the first few years, it doesn't look like a big deal, but it picks up a lot of steam later." Compounding reminds me of Sunday mornings when Grandma Chips made yeast rolls. I might not have noticed the dough rising at first, but as it continued to expand, the results seemed miraculous. No wonder money is often referred to as dough.

Compounding can seem like a curse, however, if it's connected to money that you owe. Because of compounding, when people use credit cards or take out loans, although they may pay some on their bills, the amount owed might not seem to be reduced substantially. Could anything be more frustrating than sending a $250 payment and realizing that you've only reduced your debt by $20? That's because the interest on the debt continues to compound. If you're just learning this term, take heart because you're becoming a wiser consumer.

CONSIDERING SCRIPTURE

"For there is still a vision for the appointed time; it speaks of the end, and does not lie. If it seems to tarry, wait for it; it will surely come, it will not delay."

—Habakkuk 2:3.

If the spirit moves you, read this passage aloud and write about its meaning as you become more financially literate.

_____

_____

_____

_____

_____

_____

STEP 2

Envision Your Financial Future

3

Facing Reality and Exploring Your Dreams

I love working with "Miss Beanie." Not just because she earned her nickname as a toddler when she ate her daddy's pinto beans. And not just because she doesn't care who's watching when she reaches beneath her wig to scratch her head. Or even because she once outraged her great-great-grandson at a baseball game by wearing a T-shirt that said: I'M *NOT* AN ALCOHOLIC. ALCOHOL-ICS GO TO MEETINGS. I'M A DRUNK. Most of all, I love working with Miss Beanie because during our annual telephone conference when I update her on her investments, she sometimes interrupts and says, "Keep it real, sonny."

That's what she said in 1992, when she became one of my first clients. She was sixty-nine, retired from a job as a cleaning lady at a bank, and drawing Social Security and a small monthly pension. Her husband, four years her junior, was retiring from his job as a production worker at a local tobacco plant, and she wanted me to look over his paperwork.

Despite Miss Beanie's protests that at their age they didn't have time for dreams, I persuaded her and her husband to list their values and clarify their goals. After considering these and looking over their paperwork, I suggested that her husband take the retirement cash payout of $250,000 that his company was offering instead of monthly checks totaling about $15,000 a year for the rest of his life.

As I pointed out, they lived modestly, had Medicare coverage, and could get by with pooling her Social Security benefits and his pension. That way, I continued, they could spend some of his retirement cash on the house they'd dreamed of buying and had listed in their goals. They took my advice eventually and used the company money to buy a little brick house.

I'm sad to say that life didn't turn out as they had hoped.

For two decades, her husband had smoked a pack of cigarettes a day. A year after they moved into their new home, Miss Beanie's husband was diagnosed with lung cancer. He died several months later. After the funeral, Miss Beanie clasped my hand and said, "Aaron, if we'd signed papers to get a check every month from that company, isn't it true I wouldn't be getting any more checks, now that my husband is gone?" When I nodded, she shook her head. "And I'd still be paying rent on that crummy apartment."

What does her story tell us? Certainly not that everyone should take a cash payout from an employer rather than a pension. Relatively few companies offer this option. But if you do have that choice, tread carefully. Depending on your circumstances, accepting the cash *might or might not* cost you more than you bargained for. It might mean signing away health insurance or other benefits that you need for a comfortable retirement. So please consult a financial adviser before making this or any major retirement decisions.

My advice to Miss Beanie and her husband to take the payout option was based in part on the fact that a decade earlier he had survived a bout of lung cancer. That was a reality they needed to confront, especially since he'd never quit smoking. It was difficult to raise such a delicate subject with them, but I did, and that's when they decided to take the cash payout. So although he was younger than she, there was a good chance he might die and leave her with no additional income.

Financial planning is a balance of arming yourself with realities while at the same time exploring your dreams. When you hear the word *reality*, perhaps you're thinking, "Oh, no, he's about to lower the boom and explain why I can't meet my goals." That might be one of the harsh realities for those who do not learn the nuances of financial planning, but not necessarily for you.

Think of the people whose stories have unfolded: Dr. Evelyn Greene had wiped out her retirement account and owed the government tens of thousands of dollars. Armed with financial knowledge, she recouped much of her savings and got her tax bill reduced. How about Mr. Roosevelt Haines? He delayed planning for his future, in effect losing money, because he was vaguely preparing to share his savings with a child who never existed. Putting this child out of mind freed him to work with his wife to save for their future and to pass money on to the next generation. And we can't forget Silver. She not only learned that her nieces could be educated for free, but she also earned thousands of dollars in interest-free savings. As for Miss Beanie, her life might have been changed for the worse with the stroke of a pen. None of these stories involved lucky breaks. *Chance favors the well prepared.* It is especially important to plan ahead in light of some realities.

- **Our traditional safety nets are eroding.** Corporations are increasingly cutting back on pensions, while some have defaulted on their pension obligations. And some economists are predicting that Social Security benefits will be reduced in years to come. Many of us depend on these government checks as a sole financial source after retirement. This is a mistake; it's important for us to build our own nest eggs.

- **You might live for a long time.** Lots of people think that once they quit work they have a decade or so to live. But thanks to medical breakthroughs, people are living longer than ever. It's true that life expectancy is shorter for African Americans because of exposure to higher rates of violence, lack of quality health care, and other issues related to racism and income inequality. The good news is that the more control we exert over our money, the greater our chances for enjoying a longer, healthier life. We already know that obesity and smoking are the leading causes of preventable death. What a lot of people don't realize is that conquering financial problems can give them the emotional energy they might need to change unhealthy behaviors.

- **When you're on a fixed income, you especially need to stay a step ahead of inflation.** Prices only go up, not down. You'll need a lot more money twenty years from now than you needed this year. Financial-planning strategies teach you how to factor inflation into your retirement costs and start maximizing your dollars now so you will have enough.

- **Retired people pay taxes.** Many people wrongly believe that retirement will finally free them of their debt to Uncle Sam. It would be nice if this were so, but hey, as Miss Beanie insisted, I'm keeping it real. A tax specialist will be able to suggest strategies for lowering your taxes, but that obligation will not simply disappear with retirement.

I recognize that you might have personal issues that make it particularly challenging to set goals and plan for your future. Many of my clients are going through divorces, others live with partners but are not married, and still others are struggling with illnesses or trying to help loved ones who are ill. The majority of these clients are trying to figure out how to stretch their money to meet immediate needs, and others are married to people who not only refuse to participate in financial planning but seem to go out of the way to thwart their efforts. Your difficulties might force you to put your last goal out of reach. I assume you listed your fifth goal last because you deemed the others more important. Maybe you will have to postpone your fifth goal for the time being.

It's true that there are obstacles that might keep you from reaching your goals, but I encourage you to pursue them anyway. You might not have as much money as you would like, but your *life* is rich. Among all of God's creatures, we humans are the only ones who have the capacity to think about the future. You also might be a beneficiary of a gift that God lavished on Africans, and presumably their descendants: an unrivaled optimism. Despite the myriad problems that many Africans face, they've been found to be the most optimistic people on earth.

If you do have an optimistic personality, I encourage you to use it in attaining your goals. If you aren't optimistic naturally, I encourage you to work on developing this trait.* Hope is transforming. That's the point the Reverend Jesse Jackson was making when

* One book available on this subject is *Learned Optimism: How to Change Your Mind and Your Life,* by Martin E. P. Seligman, Ph.D. (Random House, 1991).

he urged us to "keep hope alive." He realized that hopelessness could fill us with despair and apathy, cause us to lose faith in ourselves, and lead us down self-destructive paths. As you continue working through this book, you will learn to use hope like a fuel that helps you reach your goals.

Of course we could always leave our future to politicians, hoping that they'll come up with solutions to the coming Social Security and pension crises. But that's the kind of faulty thinking that led to the shame we will always remember surrounding Hurricane Katrina in New Orleans. Who was looking out for us then? Sometimes I think of Noah and how receiving word from God in advance of the flood gave him time to build his ark. Consider *In the Black* your advance warning. Wherever you are, take the time to construct a framework that will allow you to reach higher ground. I imagine Noah, once his ark landed on dry shore, throwing the doors open and saying to the others, "Now get off this boat and go for it!" In chapter 4, you'll learn to construct a financial plan that's designed to lead you to solid ground.

HELPFUL HINT

As you gather copies of financial documents, set aside time to review them for inaccuracies or terminology that you don't understand. When necessary, call company administrators and ask for corrections or explanations. You will want to get clear on when your money will be available and the terms and conditions.

BUILDING FINANCIAL LITERACY

You may remember someone "down home" using a wooden device to agitate milk or cream until it turned into butter, a process known as churning. In the financial world, *churning*—a practice used by dishonest financial professionals can slow you down as you progress toward your goals. Dishonest brokers will want to stay as far as possible from financially savvy clients who look over their accounts and who know how to put anyone who handles their investments, including retirement vehicles and insurance policies, through rigorous inquiry—something you, too, will learn as we progress through this work. But part of this process involves learning what to look out for. Selena Maranjian, columnist for the Motley Fool financial website (www.fool.com), describes churning as making a client's account "excessively active by frequent purchases and sales, primarily to generate commissions."

> **CHURNING:**
> When a broker engages in excessive trading in a client's account for the purpose of maximizing on commissions

Any financial adviser paid on the basis of generating new policies might keep moving a client's money from one company to another even if this is not to the client's advantage. The best way to guard against becoming a victim of churning is to become more financially knowledgeable. Good and decent financial professionals are all around, but those who are dishonest tend to shy away from consumers who can keep track of their transactions and who aren't shy about asking questions pertaining to their money.

"Where there is no prophecy, the people cast off restraint, but happy are those who keep the law."

—Proverbs 29:18.

If the spirit moves you, read this passage aloud and write about its meaning as you become more financially literate.

_____

_____

_____

_____

_____

_____

_____

_____

_____

4

Creating the Financial Plan
That's Right for You

When I see a self-test in a magazine, I always find it hard
to resist. They're fun when they can help me learn
more about myself. The self-test that follows is designed to identify behaviors that can help you move in a direction
that's consistent with your values and goals. There are no right or
wrong answers. If you find yourself puzzling over an answer, you're
spending too much time on it. Circle the letter that comes closest
to describing how you would react, *not* how you think you *should*
react.

1. **You win $2 million in a lottery. You would**
   A. *put off telling everyone except a tax lawyer.*
   B. *call your family and friends and celebrate the good news.*

2. **You become stranded on a desert island and you
   have with you one serving of your favorite food (a**

method for keeping it fresh for several days has been developed). You don't know when you'll be rescued. You

A. take a few bites at a time to maintain strength and guard against running out.

B. eat most of it because you're really hungry and it is your favorite food.

3. If you were involved in a reality TV show, you would want to be

A. the director, organizing everything from behind the scenes.

B. a winning contestant, becoming known and envied around the world.

4. Each evening after work, you drink a glass of wine with dinner. You want each bottle of wine to last for four nights, so you would

A. pour pretty much the same amount of wine every evening.

B. pour a tall glass the first and second nights and a medium one on the third, leaving yourself very little for the fourth night.

5. You're running for president against an opponent whose values sicken you. You have a narrow lead. An hour before the last televised debate you learn that a family member has been injured critically in an accident and you have only a short window of time to say good-bye. So you

A. tell your loved ones that family comes first . . . usually. You show up and win the debate.

B. you go home, giving the advantage to your opponent. You figure that if God means for you to win, you will.

If you enjoyed taking this self-quiz, I'm glad, because retirement planning is supposed to be enjoyable as well as helpful. Now it's time to add up your scores. How many *As* did you have? How many *Bs*? Before I tell you what your scores might suggest, I'll give you my interpretation of the answers. Record in your journal the strengths that are revealed.

1. **(Winning a Million-Dollar Lottery)** If you chose A (you would only tell a tax lawyer), you're strong-willed and not controlled by emotions. This strength will help you to move straight ahead, accomplishing one goal after another. If you chose B (call family and friends), you have a generous heart and attract loyal friends and family members. As you move toward your goals, you can turn to loved ones for emotional support.

2. **(Stranded on a Deserted Island)** If you chose A (eat a few bites at a time), you are highly disciplined. Even under extenuating circumstances, you plan for the future. That should translate into long-term savings, because even as abrupt changes occur in your life, you find a way to keep from dipping into your savings so that interest grows and compounds. If you chose B (eating it all at once), you are a risk taker and innovator—a person who comes up with new ways of doing things. You're likely to devise unique approaches to getting where you want to go and figuring out what to do next.

3. **(Involved in a Reality TV Show)** If you chose A (work as a director), you're probably a good manager. That means you'll be able to keep track of details and you're able to see

the big picture and do long-range planning. Good organization can help you remain cool-headed during life crises, so you can stay on course. If you chose B (being a winning contestant), you're confident. You believe that you have a marketable talent that you can use for earning money. As a bonus, you're probably creative, which will help you devise solutions to problems that might sidetrack others.

4. **(Drinking a Bottle of Wine Over Four Nights)** If you chose A (pouring the same amount each night), you're diligent. Remember the fable of the ant and the grasshopper? The ant gathered and stored wheat for the winter, while the grasshopper danced and sang. In this scenario, you're the ant, mindful that putting aside a little at a time can add up to enough. If you chose B (leaving little for yourself at the end), you have a strongly developed sense of abundance, the belief that you'll figure out how to have enough. Maybe you'll add juice to the last glass of wine, making it taste like sangria. That attitude will be helpful if you need to cut back in some areas in order to meet your goals.

5. **(Family Member's Accident Just Before Your Presidential Debate)** If you chose A (showed up for the debate and won), you're a fierce competitor and believe winning is most important. There's not much that can stop you from pursuing your goals. You're not sentimental, which can be helpful in financial matters. Making money often calls for making tough decisions. If you chose B (went to see your loved one), you might be deeply faithful. Turning to God in prayer will give you the strength that you need to endure and the assurance of what you're hoping for in the future.

And now, here's how to understand your score. Please record:

Number of A responses: _____
Number of B responses: _____

If you got four or more As, you value autonomy. This means that you're good at governing yourself. Of course you, too, might turn to God for strength, but the opinions of others don't hold too much sway over you. You have a strong sense of yourself and what you need to do to succeed.

If you got four or more Bs, you value the collaborative approach. You are comfortable turning to others to elicit support and ideas and often create synergistic relationships, which means that through interaction with others you achieve more beneficial results than you might working individually. In emergencies, you navigate challenges by seeking the opinions of others before making a final decision.

If you scored a mix of As and Bs, you have a combination of the traits identified in autonomous and collaborative personality types, which means you're flexible. You can work independently as well as cooperate with others to seek solutions. Confident and caring, you enjoy devising creative strategies to get you where you want to go. If thrown off track, you will display a stubborn determination to get back on board.

As you can see, this personality quiz has highlighted specific positive traits that help you operate in the world. Now you will want to link those traits to the values and goals you established in the first and second steps of this process.

Let me help by encouraging you to picture yourself proceeding along a road. You've been around awhile, so travel is nothing new to you, but this is the first time you know where you're going. Continuing isn't always easy, so you draw upon particular resources—this may be a reservoir of well-being that comes from within, from your environment, or both, depending upon your needs. When you reach a personal-goal milestone, you become jubilant.

Don't stop now. Record the strengths that were delineated in the self-test. For instance, those who fit the autonomous model might write: "I have a strong will, I am highly disciplined, and I know how to plan ahead. I'm a good manager and keep track of details. I'm a fierce competitor."

Those who fit the collaborative model might write: "I am generous and have strong connections to family and friends. I'm a risk taker, innovative, confident, and creative. I have a strongly developed sense of abundance and a deep faith in God." Those with a mix of traits will have all the more to write in the spaces provided below.

Strengths That Will Help Me Meet My Financial Goals

1. _____

2. _____

3. _____

4. _____

5. _____

If you notice that you have never or seldom demonstrated the traits you've identified, make checkmarks beside them. These might be gifts lying dormant within you, which you will have an opportunity to develop along your journey. In pursuing your goals you will find plenty of opportunities for self-enhancement.

When you've finished writing down your strengths, read the words aloud. These are the characteristics that will help you meet your goals.

When I first met Pierre François, he was twenty-seven years old. As my client, he identified three goals he wanted to pursue. First and foremost, he wanted to save for his daughter's education. Next he wanted to buy a home. Third, he wanted to put away money for retirement. (You would be impressed at how many young people have figured out that because of compounding, saving modest amounts regularly over twenty and thirty years will allow them to retire as millionaires.)

It wasn't as if Mr. François had lots of money. He was born in Haiti and had recently immigrated to the United States. When I began working with him, he wasn't fluent in English, so I didn't learn much about his life. He worked as an aide in a nearby preschool, and this allowed him to take his infant daughter along. For our first session, Mr. François showed up carrying his baby girl strapped to his chest. When I asked about the baby's mother, Mr. François gave me a sad look, and I didn't press.

He explained that he wanted to make the most of his money. He earned $1,000 a month, after taxes, and he was willing to save half of that amount every month. He and his daughter lived frugally. They shared a room in a rooming house for $200 a month, and Mr. François walked everywhere because he didn't own a car. After he began working with me, he set up a street table selling incense. Like a lot of people who are determined to reach their goals, rather than dipping into savings to help pay for extra costs, he found a way to increase his income. Mr. François definitely fit the autonomous model, showing independence and steely determination.

It took me seven years to discover what motivated Mr. François. By that time, he'd met his goal of making a down payment on a house. He had followed my advice and invested money he earned from his incense sales into a mix of stocks, bonds, and mutual funds and allowed his profits to compound. In this manner, his investment of $48,000 grew to $71,000.* He spent one third of that money to secure his new home, and he invited me to attend the closing.

As usual Mr. François's daughter accompanied him. By now she was in the third grade. They were accompanied by a lovely young woman whom Mr. François introduced as his child's mother and his wife. She had arrived from Haiti recently. It had taken Mr. François seven years to be able to afford for her to join them. I believe that his desire to reunite his family motivated him to reach his goals and kept him moving forward.

What will help you progress? I have included some suggestions:

- **Ask God for support.** Progress can be divinely inspired through prayer and discernment. Talk to God about your goals and ask for guidance.

- **Break down goals.** Once you've identified your goals, write down starting and continuing points. For instance, if your goal is to improve your health, you might write, "Walk three times a week." Then come up with another, smaller goal that helps you progress. Plan around these goals. The chart on the next page may help you keep on track.

* Results may vary. The experience of one investor might not be representative of stock market behavior in general.

Goals			
Starting Point			
I know I'm moving forward because...			
Another sign of progress is...			

- **Visualize what you want.** Pick up a copy of *Essence, O, Ebony, American Legacy,* or *Black Enterprise* and cut out photos that portray our array of beauty. Find images of families and graduates, homes, and retirement communities, whatever fits within the context of your goals. Paste those pictures inside the cover of this book or your journal so you can continue to visualize where you're going.

- **Change your belief system.** Write affirmations that empower you in your pursuit of your goals. Keep your words positive and direct. It can be as simple as "Every day I'm adding to my savings." Repeat your affirmation aloud several times a day.

My Affirmations

○ _____

○ _____

○ _____

- **Make success feel real.** Write a letter congratulating yourself for having met a particular goal. Mail the letter to yourself. When you reach the goal, open the letter and read it aloud.

- **Party.** Host an inexpensive potluck or picnic to celebrate reaching a goal.

- **Maya Angelou yourself.** Read her autobiography, *I Know Why the Caged Bird Sings*, or her poem "And Still I Rise." Either one of these literary achievements will stir your emotions and launch you forward.

- **Let music inspire you.** Listen to an inspirational song or belt it out during difficult times. Artists and titles might include: Gloria Gaynor's "I Will Survive," Bobby McFerrin's "Don't Worry, Be Happy," Louis Armstrong's "What a Wonderful World," Bob Marley's "No Woman, No Cry," Aretha Franklin's "Think (Freedom)," and "Amazing Grace" by any number of artists. Record titles that come to mind that boost your spirits.

My Inspirational Songs

○ _____

○ _____

○ _____

- **Practice gratitude.** Thank God for every success and for every new day. Study your financial plan regularly. As an expression of your goals, it will give direction to your efforts. Goals can serve as crucial psychological triggers that will help spur you to action. You are poised at the starting line. Wherever you have been in the past, whatever missteps you may have made, you cannot turn the clock back, but you can start again. By writing down a plan, you have already increased your likelihood of following it through.

With the second step completed, you can move on to exploring factors that can foster or obstruct your progress, so you can change and grow along with your balance sheet.

HELPFUL HINT
Get comfortable with financial lingo by reading information at www.mymoney.gov, a government website offering the basics of financial planning. You also may want to subscribe to _Black Enterprise, Kiplinger's,_ or _Money_ or read them at a public library or online.

BUILDING FINANCIAL LITERACY

With an eye on expanding your financial knowledge, start taking note of the products you use regularly. It's likely that many are produced by companies that impact our economy. If you've ever played poker, you might recall that the chip worth the most is colored blue. In financial terms, _blue-chip stocks_ are issued by established, highly respected companies such as Coca-Cola and Wal-Mart. Companies such as these have a history of earnings and dividend payments, and investments in these highly valued companies tend to be expensive.* Because of their reputation for reliability, many view blue-chip stocks as highly suitable for retirement portfolios.

> **BLUE-CHIP STOCKS:**
> Shares or stocks issued by financially fit companies that are known for selling quality products

CONSIDERING SCRIPTURE

"Happy are those whose transgression is forgiven, whose sin is covered." **—Psalm 32:1.**
If the spirit moves you, read this passage aloud and write about its meaning in your life as you become more financially literate.

_____

_____

_____

_____

_____

* Historically, a portfolio that includes blue-chip stocks tends to be less volatile than those that feature more speculative equities. However, blue-chip stocks are no guarantee of favorable results, and they involve risk, including loss of principal.

STEP 3

Work Your Money

5

Paying Yourself First

Our community and my practice is made up of a diverse blend of people from all income levels, including men and women who have built impressive fortunes. But if I focused solely on the well-to-do, I'd be distorting who we are and doing you a tremendous disservice, because you might not see yourself represented. I don't want to give anyone the impression that funding a retirement is out of reach.

Moderate-income clients often seek me out at the recommendation of friends or family or after hearing me speak at employer-sponsored workshops. Quite a few of these clients head their own households. With more than 50 percent of black women raising children in households in which the father is absent; with only one third of our women likely to marry in their lifetimes versus twice as many in the general population; and with more than half of our children born into impoverished households, these struggling parents cannot and should not be ignored.

Don't get me wrong. This chapter is designed to help men and women at every income level and marital status. At this point I'm focusing on single black mothers who were once struggling for the same reason that authors of the Bible included stories about widows. Both groups of women were marginalized in their societies. In ancient Israel the women considered most valuable were unmarried virgins, due to their procreative potential and because they could bring property into a marriage in the form of a dowry. Widows, on the other hand, especially those without sons, were considered worthless.

Today we live in more politically correct times, but low-earning, single black mothers are rarely accorded the respect they deserve for juggling the responsibilities of both parents with modest resources. That's unfortunate, because like the scriptural widows, they can inspire and motivate us. If they can succeed, then it will no longer be easy to make excuses about why we cannot.

Before I tell you about Kendra Brown and Sandra Armstrong, I'd like you to participate in an exercise that requires only your imagination. For a few minutes, imagine that an elderly cousin has left you a crumbling house, and you climb up to the attic to look around. Sorting through boxes and trunks, you discover a chest filled with diamonds, black opals, emeralds, and pearls. You have the contents appraised and learn that you are rich. What a relief to realize that you can now take care of all your responsibilities.

Picture yourself reaching into the chest to hand a pile of those gems to the college of your child's (or grandchild's) choice to assure that he or she gets an education and fares well in the future. You can also move to a new house now, a place better suited to your improved financial status, so you hand over another pile of gems to the mortgage company. One of the pleasures of wealth is no more phone calls from debt collectors; another pile of gems is accorded to them. You might also increase your tithe to your church. The new house needs furniture and a few repairs, and you keep handing the gems over until finally you've met all your obligations. It's a good feeling—for a while. The next time you open that treasure chest, you're stunned to find that you have only a few gems left, not nearly enough to survive on for retirement. Once again, your future is cloudy.

You might argue that you didn't do anything wrong. You made a good investment by buying a house. You don't owe anyone, and you're still glad that you donated to the church. And wasn't it right to provide for your child's education? *Of course,* you're right. But why are you left in a precarious situation?

Enough with imagining this reversal in fortunes; it's too disheartening.

You might be thinking the exercise was a time waster, that you would never be crazy enough to give away all those gems and that you would definitely leave enough for yourself. But would you?

What if this distribution of gems had occurred over a longer period, such as during your work history? If you have been collecting your financial documents, look at your Social Security statement and turn to the section that reads "Your Earning Records at a Glance." In this section you'll find a listing of the years you worked and the amount of money you have earned. Add up the total. Let's say the amount comes to $200,000 or half a million or three million.

God has provided you with the energy and talent to perform various jobs, and the dollars you earned using these gifts represent the gems you have earned during your lifetime. The question is, How many of those gems, symbolizing your earned income, have you put aside for yourself? If the amount seems insignificant, then your behavior might well reflect the gem-give-away.

The purpose of this exercise is not to make you feel foolish. And I'm not suggesting that you should let your bills go unpaid, refuse to help your children secure an education, or stop paying tithe. I am saying that you shouldn't leave yourself out of the picture. My coauthor,

Brenda Lane Richardson, was startled to realize that although she had been careful to budget her money, paying bills on time, recording details of where her money was going—gas, electric, water, auto insurance, kids' tuition, et cetera—she had never added her own and her husband's name to the list.

What I'm advocating is called paying yourself. Some people think it's the same as saving money, but they miss the point. "Saving" can feel like drudgery; it's what you do because you feel you should—or else. "Paying yourself" is a silent declaration that you are holding on to a portion of what you earn, because you deserve it. Can you think of anyone who would be willing to work for you without pay, year after year, without financial remuneration? I assume your answer is no, so why would you be willing to do that to yourself? You work for yourself, don't you? So pay yourself.

Plenty of my clients are good at this without any prompting, while others have resisted this behavior because they were still stuck on the idea of *saving*. It's a word that can carry a lot of emotional baggage. Maybe you had a relative who scrimped through life without having any fun at all, always worrying about saving. Perhaps you decided you'd never live that way, and so you spent without concern. You might have felt all the more determined to spend if someone shamed you, warning that you'd wind up destitute by not saving. As money has passed through your life, you might have blamed yourself for spending lavishly, only deepening your sense of shame and leading you to spend more. Now is the time to stop looking back and start looking forward.

When I meet people and they tell me about their financial goals, whatever those goals are, I can usually gauge right away whether they will ever get where they want to go. It doesn't matter if they earn $30,000 or $300,000—all they have to tell me is whether they're saving money. If they have children and aren't saving at least 10 percent of their income; if they're childless or empty-nesters and aren't saving at least 20 percent, I know that they haven't mastered the discipline of saving, and therefore they don't have much chance of realizing their dreams. So from this day forward, no matter what else is going on in your life, get serious about setting something aside for your goals. It's a habit that can be learned, especially if you have the money deducted from your pay-check or checking account automatically.

Reframing the savings concept by thinking of it as paying your-self is a way of shoring up your sense of worth. And a growing num-ber of us agree. In a 2006 report, the Joint Center for Political and Economic Studies, a research group focusing on policy issues con-cerning African Americans, found a trend toward greater savings among African Americans overall. But black women forty-five and older (37 percent versus 29 percent of the general population) re-port feeling that the future is so uncertain it's pointless to plan fi-nancially. Among that age group, 25 percent (versus 41 percent of the general population) are less likely to always save part of their monthly income, according to a 2005 AARP Foundation Women's Leadership Circle Study. I say to them and to you, do not despair. It is not too late.

When it comes to retirement planning and meeting your goals, it's not how much you have. It's about the habits you develop from this point on. The good news is that doing almost nothing can move you forward. Since that probably sounds like a contradiction, I'd better explain myself. I'm a big fan of automatic. I like walking through doors that I don't have to push because they swing open automatically. And it's a small relief to know that I won't have to wonder when to update my computer antivirus software because the company offers automatic updates. It's the same idea with my car, which is equipped with an automatic transmission. Life is busy, so when the situation allows, I want to put minimal effort into getting where I want to go.

If you're heading toward your retirement goals, in part by paying yourself, you will be glad to know that there's a plan already in place to help you get there automatically. Short of finding a treasure chest, there are few alternatives better than *tax-deferred retirement savings plans*, which allow you to participate through employer-sponsored automatic salary deductions. You can decide how much you want to pay yourself and how to invest the money. The 2006 Pension Protection Act encourages employers to enroll workers automatically in 401(k)-type plans. (These should not be confused with deferred compensation plans, which are offered mainly to highly paid executives to shelter excess income. These types of accounts cannot be rolled over into qualified plans.)

> **TAX-DEFERRED RETIREMENT SAVINGS PLAN:**
> 401(k)-type plans that allow you to save for retirement through employer-sponsored automatic salary deductions

If you work for a company or organization that signs you up automatically for a tax-deferred retirement savings plan, one of the worst decisions you might make is to opt out of the plan. This is one time when inertia—the tendency most of us feel from time to time to remain still and do nothing—can work to your advantage. Not only do these plans help you save money, but depending on the type of plan you choose, they may offer immediate and tax-deferred savings on the money that you contribute. Tax-deferred retirement savings plans take different forms, depending on your employer.

TYPES OF TAX-DEFERRED RETIREMENT SAVINGS PLANS

- **401(k).** Corporations as well as small businesses offer these plans to their employees and sometimes match contributions or kick in a percentage of what the employee pays. Turn your back on that money and you might be losing tens of thousands of dollars over decades. Beware of early withdrawals (before you're fifty-nine and a half) that will incur heavy state and federal taxes and penalties. The benefit of having that threat hanging over your head is that it tends to dissuade you from dipping into these accounts. You can borrow against this money, but for the sake of allowing your money to compound, you're almost always better off letting it grow.

- **403(b).** Similar to the 401(k), these retirement plans are offered by nonprofit organizations, such as universities and charitable organizations.

- **457(b).** Employees of state and some local governments can contribute to this tax-advantaged retirement plan or a 401(a) plan.

- **Thrift Savings Plan (TSP).** Civilians employed by the U.S. government and the armed services can save for retirement through this plan.

- **Keogh.** These plans allow the self-employed to save a specific percentage of income/profit each year.

- **solo(k).** Those who run a one-person business can use this retirement plan to shelter income. One drawback is that there's a lot of paperwork involved, so you might want to consider consulting a registered financial counselor before enrolling. You also can choose to have the bank deduct the money automatically from your checking account.

From here on, I'll call these and other tax-advantaged accounts "401(k)-type plans."

WATCH OUT FOR HIDDEN 401(K)-TYPE PLAN FEES

You will have to pay administrative costs on any 401(k)-type account. If you've opened one, call your fund and ask what you're being charged annually. Administrative fees include everything from investment expenses to education seminars. Along with asking for cost breakdowns, be sure to ask what percentage of your savings is being deducted in fees. An extra 1 percent can cost you plenty. For instance, if a twenty-five-year-old saved $25,000 and never added another penny to a 401(k)-type plan that earned a hypothetical rate of 7 percent interest for thirty years, and with administrative fees of .5 percent compounded monthly and deducted each year, by the time he reached fifty-five, his account would be worth $174,795. But if administrative fees had been 1.5 percent a year—one point higher—his account would be worth $129,685. That's $45,110 less over thirty years.

The higher the fees in your 401(k)-type account, the more it will cost you. If the fees are too high, speak with an administrator in your human resources department about changing or renegotiating fees. If you want more information about how to protect your savings, get the pamphlet *A Look at 401(k) Fees* by calling toll-free (866) 444-3272 or go online to www.aarp.org/money/financial_planning. Under "Retirement Planning," click "Fees, Fees, and More 401(k) Fees."

GET HELP IN MANAGING YOUR 401(K)-TYPE INVESTMENTS

A 2007 Charles Schwab study found that employees who got professional advice about selecting mutual funds in their 401(k)-type accounts earned 3 percent higher returns annually than workers who made choices on their own. Three percent may not sound like a whole lot, but over a period of ten to thirty years, that can mean leaving thousands of dollars on the table. Here's my advice: Get as much as you can from the money you pay yourself.

TAKE YOUR 401(K)-TYPE PLAN WITH YOU IF YOU CHANGE JOBS

After leaving a job, you may want to leave your 401(k)-type money in place long enough to decide what to do with it. Over time, however, with consolidation in mind, it may be best to arrange to have your money rolled directly over into your new employer's 401(k)-type plan, for the purpose of consolidation. If you're tempted to dip into that money, remember that you risk having to pay taxes and penalties, as illustrated by Dr. Greene's story in the introduction of this book.

Sometimes automatic savings plans seem like such a good deal that people view them suspiciously. I find this to be the case especially among my lowest-income clients, who justifiably point out that they need every dime they can get their hands on. Here are the stories of two clients.

Profile: Kendra Brown, a forty-nine-year-old mother of one, works for a drugstore chain and earns $270 a week before taxes. Her company offered 401(k) plans with a matching incentive.

Ms. Brown argued vociferously when I suggested that she sign up for the 401(k). "I don't have an extra penny," she insisted. She easily qualified as my most reluctant client, and I understood why. Right after we began working together in 1997, her live-in boyfriend left her for her best friend, which left Ms. Brown holding the bag on the entire rent payment and support of their son.

She took my advice grudgingly and signed on to the company 401(k) plan. Five years later, when a niece got into an accident and Ms. Brown wanted to help pay medical fees, she called to say she was pulling her "little bit of money" from her 401(k) account. I later learned that she grew so distracted that she never filled out the withdrawal paperwork. The doctor agreed to being paid in installments. When I saw her again, she was caring for her elderly mother and still bemoaning her deduction, even though she opted to increase it after she received a raise.

A funny thing happened on the way to Ms. Brown's retirement. Over a period of ten years, the $118 a month that was deposited automatically into her account compounded into $21,588.* At age fifty-nine and a half, in 2007, she used half of that amount to start a dressmaking business. A year later she was earning enough to hire a bookkeeper—her son. She still runs into his father, her ex-boyfriend, who by now has deserted Ms. Brown's former best friend too.

The bottom line: *Retirement plans make saving easy by deducting money automatically.*

Many people feel wary about 401(k)-type plans because they fear market fluctuations, but financial literacy can calm their jitters. It helps to understand that investing in a retirement savings account doesn't mean giving up control of your money. More and more companies are offering 401(k)-type plans with what is referred to as "target date" or "life-cycle" funds. Here's how these work. As the target date for retirement approaches, the money is moved automatically from stocks and bonds to conservative or "cash" investment accounts—CDs or money market—so people aren't starting retire-

---

* Results may vary. The experience of one investor might not be representative of stock market behavior in general.

ment feeling like they're behind before they start. Many pre-retirees lost out during the stock market declines, beginning in 2008, because they did not understand the importance of taking this kind of action. This is one example of how financial literacy can improve the quality of your life. If you don't have this option, talk to your plan administrator and ask that cash accounts be made available.

Younger workers with a low tolerance for seeing negative return balances on their retirement statements might also want to reallocate funds to more conservative accounts, which they have the option to do. They should be aware that they aren't so much as "losing money" when the stock market goes down as they are buying into companies at bargain prices. If you have more than five years to go before retirement, you probably have enough time to wait for the markets to recover, and then the bargains you purchased are likely to be worth more. I'll have a lot of information to share later concerning investments. For the time being, rest assured that the more you know about finances, the more you can earn.

Profile: Sandra Armstrong, a fifty-seven-year-old divorcee, is the mother of two teenagers and is employed as a domestic worker. Her average take-home pay is $1,600 a month.

When Ms. Armstrong began working with me in 1994, she confided that she wasn't paying taxes because her employers paid her "under the table." I explained that not only were they breaking the law—her employers were required to report earnings over a certain amount a year for domestic workers—but they were doing her a disservice. As I explained, if her earnings weren't reported, she couldn't qualify for future Social Security benefits. I suggested that she convince her employers to start paying a portion of her Social Security, Medicare, federal and state unemployment, and disability taxes, and that she should start filing an income tax return.

She seemed amused by the idea. "I'd never get the people I work for to agree to all that stuff. They'd think I'd lost my mind."

On the contrary, I told her, they would think she'd come to her senses. She'd worked for two of her clients for five years, and neither of them would be eager to let her go, I added. She was still chuckling when she left.

The next time I saw her, she said she had asked her longtime clients about reporting her earnings. "One of them had the nerve to fire me." Ms. Armstrong gave me an outraged look and added, "That's okay. I got two new jobs and I asked for more money. I'm gonna start paying that payroll and income tax."

Thirteen years later Ms. Armstrong retired at the age of seventy and qualified for a monthly Social Security check for the rest of her life. She also received money regularly from a self-funded pension financed with an IRA rollover. She says she's enjoying her retirement.

The bottom line: *Social Security can be a lifeline, especially for low-income workers. However, it is not intended to be a sole source of retirement income. Instead, it is meant to supplement pensions, insurance, savings, and other investments accumulated during our working years.*

Here are some other suggestions for growing your savings.

- **Check "yes" on automatic deduction raises.** If you work at a job that offers the so-called "autopilot" feature, boosting your deduction automatically from maybe 10 to 12 percent in your fifth year of employment, don't overrule this feature. You'll save lots more over the long run. In October 2006, *Money* magazine reported on an experiment at one company that found automatic contribution hikes raised average savings rates from 3.5 percent to 11.6 percent.

- **Don't dip into retirement savings to send your kids to college.** As *Kiplinger's* Winter 2007 "Success with

Your Money" guide suggests, you don't want to even consider it. If necessary, find a less expensive school for your child. Money borrowed from a 401(k)-type account doesn't build income, and you have to repay the loan in five years or risk paying tax penalties. On top of all that, if you change jobs, you have to repay the money right away or risk paying taxes and penalties.

- **Be wary of on-the-job investment advice.** You might get some great ideas from advisers hired by your employer, but before you make major financial decisions, consult an adviser whom you have chosen to look out for your specific interests.

- **Play catch-up.** If you're fifty or older and behind in your goals, double up on retirement savings, if possible, contributing the maximum allowed by law. How much you need to save will be discussed later. For now, just get into the habit.

- **Generate more income.** You can't squeeze money from a stone. If your income doesn't leave room for you to meet your responsibilities and pay yourself, come up with income-producing ideas. Creative/collaborative types might start a small business with a few friends, while autonomous personalities might prefer efforts such as collecting used books and reselling them. If you enjoy baking or cooking, sell your goods. Perhaps you can subcontract skills that you use full-time. My co-author, Brenda Lane Richardson, earned cash to pay for graduate school by writing book proposals and soon had more work than she could handle.

- **Bully yourself into the habit of paying yourself.** If after making these efforts you're still paying everyone else except yourself, go on the Internet and get the names of the heads of corporations that receive your money. Read about them and then ask yourself how it feels to be paying them everything and leaving yourself nothing. Tape a photo of yourself inside this book, and when you see it, promise to pay yourself first.

- **Schedule "abundance days."** Celebrate God's generosity by having once-a-week abundance days when you don't purchase anything; dedicate the day's worth of salary toward debts or to pay yourself; and prepare meals made from canned and freezer foods that you already have. Abundance cooking draws upon your creative skills.

- **Take care when you shop.** Shop with a list, and keep a tally of all the items you don't buy but were tempted to. Take the money you saved yourself or even half that amount, and put it into your retirement account. This is fun for those more autonomous, disciplined types, and it works well for everyone.

- **Choose a role model.** Tape a photo inside the cover of this book of someone you love and admire who models the pay-yourself attribute. Or you can download a photo of Oseola McCarthy, the low-income laundress from Mississippi. In 1995, at age eighty-seven, Miss McCarthy made headlines when she donated $150,000 of her savings to the University of Southern Mississippi to fund scholarships for African Americans. Her gift inspired others to give to the university for the same cause. The secret to her savings success, Miss McCarthy explained before she died in 1999, was that once she put her money into savings accounts, "I never would take any of it out. I just put it in. It just accumulated." Over the years she invested her accumulated wealth into CDs, conservative mutual funds, and other accounts, while living frugally. She maintained good health by walking everywhere and not buying a car. Miss McCarthy also left bequests for her church and several relatives.

- **Cultivate gratitude.** You may notice that I appreciate the concept of gratitude. I stress this principle because God is gracious, and for this I am grateful. In this spirit I try to refrain from badmouthing your income, and thank God for the energy and talent that helps you earn it. Pray that you'll remain open to new opportunities that will allow you to generate more.

In the next chapter you'll have an opportunity to develop a wealth-building habit that helps you keep track of what you earn.

HELPFUL HINT

Get a copy of your credit report, which includes information from three companies—Equifax, Experian, and TransUnion—and is also available to potential employers, landlords, credit card companies, mortgage brokers, and anyone else who wants to run a financial background check on you. Your credit report details the amounts you owe, your attempts to get new credit, whether you have been sued and/or arrested, and whether you have filed for bankruptcy.

Don't let shame stop you from sending for this important document. By seeing the report you will know whether there are any mistakes to clear up, and whether you need to raise your FICO score, a three-digit number that ranges from 400 to 850. Lenders use this score to determine the interest rate you will be charged for major loans, such as for a home or a car. If you find yourself panicking, remember that credit scores and histories can be rebuilt. To apply for your free report online, go to www.annualcreditreport.com. This is the only authorized source for accessing your annual free credit report online. You can also phone (877) 322-8228 to request a brochure, or for a mail-in form go online to: www.annualcreditreport.com/cra/requestformfinal.pdf.

BUILDING FINANCIAL LITERACY

For some, the word *bonds* conjures thoughts of baseball home-run king Barry Bonds. In the financial world, bonds are IOUs, promises to repay a sum of money, and they're sold by federal, state, and local governments, corporations and other institutions that promise to repay the principal and interest on a specified date. Bonds are popular investments for people building wealth for retirement. The income they generate is set when a bond is sold, so it's designed to pay the same amount. Bonds are considered less risky than stocks, but they do hold a degree of risk.*

---

* The risk of bonds involve interest rates, credit, and inflation. Long-term bonds are more exposed to interest-rate risk than short-term bonds. Lower-rated bonds may offer higher yields in return for more credit risk.

"But remember the Lord your God, for it is He who gives you power to get wealth, so that He may confirm His covenant that He swore to your ancestors, as He is doing today." —Deuteronomy 8:18.

If the spirit moves you, read this passage aloud and write about its meaning as you become more financially literate.

_____

_____

_____

_____

_____

_____

_____

_____

_____

6

Getting a Handle on Your Spending

Don't you think this is a waste of time for someone like me?"
Will McHenry, sixty-three, self-made multimillionaire
and owner of fast-food franchises, had shown lots of enthusiasm in the early steps of retirement planning. But the idea of
recording his personal expenditures stopped him in his tracks.

What was important, he argued, was that he had more than
enough money to support his thirty-five-year-old wife, Sherri
McHenry, and their two-year-old son, and lots left over to provide
occasional help to his two young-adult children from his first marriage. He stood, opening his wallet and displaying a wad of crisp
hundred-dollar bills, and said dramatically, "When I was a high
school dropout, mopping floors at McDonalds', I swore that when I
hit the big time I'd never worry about money again."

Mrs. McHenry had remained quiet during his protestations, but
now she spoke up. "Is there any reason you don't want me to know
where your money goes?"

Short and slender, Mr. McHenry spun on his heel like a bantam rooster. "Haven't I given you everything you've ever wanted? I even left my wife for you."

Mrs. McHenry said in a soft, accusatory tone, "She's not your wife anymore."

It would be easy to think that rich people like the McHenrys have little in common with you and your financial situation, but you'll find universal truths in their story. Every once in a while in my office, tensions surface between couples, especially when we touch upon specifics about money. And tracking expenditures is about as specific as it gets. Maybe the word *tracking* makes people feel defensive because of its negative connotation. It brings to mind suspicion, secrets, and invaded privacy. When it comes to money, tracking our expenses will lead us to uncover the truth, although no judgment need follow.

Tracking is beneficial in retirement planning, because it allows you to stop speaking in generalities, such as: "I spend about eighty dollars a month on gas." When you're finished tracking, you will be able to speak with authority about your own financial life. Before you begin, it's important to understand why uncovering the truth about your spending patterns might make you feel uncomfortable. If not, you'll never truly commit, and you'll "forget" to record some expenditures or make excuses about being too busy, thus undermining your efforts. Generalities can keep you in a state of denial.

Only about a tenth of my clients are as wealthy as the McHenrys, but they serve to remind us that the extent of wealth has little bearing on the emotional power money has over us. Fights over money rank among the top reasons couples break up. Even when relationships survive the discontent, couples might continue to disagree.

According to a 2006 Pew Research Center study, 38 percent of married adults report arguing over money "often" or "sometimes."

High income doesn't insulate people from this problem. According to the study, when it comes to money arguments, there's relatively little difference between couples earning $100,000 or more annually (38 percent report arguing over money) versus those earning less than $30,000 (45 percent say they argue). The expense of raising kids seems to stoke the fires no matter what the income, because among couples with children eighteen and under, 45 percent report marital discord over finances.

Couples don't often argue over money in front of me, but at least a third of my married clients plan their retirement individually, without any input from their spouse. No one knows what goes on in a marriage better than the two people who are in it. Sometimes working individually is a silent statement about the lack of commitment in a relationship. Whatever their reason, I take my clients as they come, and I am always grateful that they're working with me, whether on their own or as a team. When we first start working together, however, I encourage married clients to consider whether working without their spouses is in their best financial interests.

For instance, you might have a partner who withdraws money from a retirement savings account, and that could cost you plenty. If you file a joint tax return, both of you will be expected to pay penalties to the state and federal governments. The same goes for taking out a second mortgage on a house. The point is that your spouse's financial decisions will impact the amount of money you have available jointly for retirement.

Sometimes clients will insist that their relationships are in pretty good shape but add that they're accustomed to making their own decisions. Often I hear women say, "I'm not going to let some man tell me how to spend my money." Men say, "She's not my mother. I don't have to report to her."

Women will tell me that when they were children, their mothers warned, "Don't tell a man everything. Put a little something aside for yourself." Men say they were warned that some women would try to take them for everything they've got. And men and women alike say they were raised to believe that it's foolish to "put their business in the street." Those attitudes about the importance of maintaining secrecy around money run so deep that a lot of my single clients resist tracking their expenditures, because they're afraid of seeing the details of their own spending habits. It's as if they're so accustomed to keeping secrets, they want to keep their own money secrets from themselves.

As for Mr. McHenry, he'd shared with me some details about his hardscrabble beginnings. I knew he'd left his troubled home at the age of fourteen and dropped out of school when the other kids teased him about being short and not having clean clothes to wear. I'm not a psychologist of course, but as a former sociology major, I've read about how an individual's experiences shape personality traits. In *Childhood and Society*, renowned psychoanalyst Erik Erikson explained that people who have been shamed a great deal can become secretly determined to get away with behaviors that others cannot see.

Mrs. McHenry was angry about her husband's secretive nature concerning money. I later learned that an earlier disagreement over spending was the catalyst that brought them to my office in the first place. After their little contretemps, he left suddenly, insisting that he had a business appointment. But he said he would record every penny he spent. Mrs. McHenry stayed behind, ostensibly to make another appointment. Before leaving, she said they had decided to start working with me after she discovered her husband had spent $120,000 on his oldest daughter's wedding.

"I know we can afford it. I don't mind the cost," she said. "I hate being kept in the dark about what we have. I used to earn a good living as a principal. After I gave birth, my husband asked me to stay home until our son was in kindergarten. I was happy to, but I'm not earning a salary anymore. I may not have been rich, but I always put money aside for the future, and I don't plan to stop now. How can we know what we will need if we don't figure out what's going out and what's coming in?"

She'd made an important point. No matter how little or how much you have, your future depends on figuring out where your money is going. Not tracking it is akin to trying to move ahead through unfamiliar terrain by looking through a pair of unfocused binoculars. You track money to create financial clarity. Some clients love recording their expenditures because the outcome can be revelatory. Others are turned off by the idea.

If that's your response, do a little writing about it, especially if you feel ashamed of how you've handled money. Some people find it helpful to write letters to the Lord, explaining how they're feeling and why. They start to remember incidents from childhood, including memories of their parents and money. Many of my clients use these letter-writing exercises to pray for a better outcome and then visualize change.

Date _____

Dear Lord,

_____

_____

_____

_____

_____

_____

_____

_____

_____

Keep writing until you've let yourself off the hook. If you need more room, continue writing in your financial journal. But refrain from blaming yourself. The average American spends about 10 percent more than he earns, with many spending a lot more than that. If that's the case for you, remind yourself that you're taking action now to ensure that your money starts flowing in the right direction—toward your future.

I don't know what kind of conversations the McHenrys engaged in after our meeting, but the next time I spoke with them, during a telephone appointment, Mr. McHenry was cooperative. He explained that they had been tracking their spending and tallying up amounts but that they hadn't had time to share the results with each other.

Mrs. McHenry suggested they read their lists aloud. Her personal and household expenses included $6,000 a month for their mortgage, $40,000 a year salary and expenses for a live-in nanny, $20,000 a year for entertainment, $6,000 for a personal trainer, $30,000 for a housekeeper, $18,000 for clothing, shoes, and accessories, and $7,000 for auto expenses.

When she finished reading from her list, Mr. McHenry didn't complain about the quarter-of-a-million-dollar-a-year expenditures.

In fact, he asked his wife whether she needed to increase her allowance. The pleasant atmosphere changed when he started on his list. His wife laughed when he said he gave away $200 a month on tips, but she didn't sound happy to hear that despite paying a generous monthly alimony to his ex-wife, he'd also started paying $48,000 a year for her mortgage on a retirement condo in South Carolina.

He said defensively, "She stuck with me when I had nothing, and she deserves it."

"I'm not suggesting that she doesn't," his wife said in a highly controlled voice.

Perhaps embarrassed about their spat, the two seemed determined to remain civil. Whatever the degree of Mrs. McHenry's displeasure at having been kept in the dark about her husband's expenditures, I hoped it was some comfort that at least now she knew the details. In the weeks to come they were able to figure out their cash flow: how much money was coming in and how much was going out. With this information, they were able to move through the planning process. Mr. McHenry had used this retirement-planning step, tracking expenses, to admit the truth.

Many clients use this step to wipe the slate clean. Leslie, fifty-nine, a graphic artist, whose combined household income, including her live-in boyfriend's earnings, totaled $53,000, was tired of racing to pick up the phone before her boyfriend realized that bill collectors were calling. "I also rented a post office box and got the bills diverted so he wouldn't see them," said Leslie. "He didn't know we were in debt, but we had terrible fights over money. He must have sensed that something was wrong." When they began planning for retirement, Leslie told him the truth and he was furious. But they hung in there, tracking their money and paying off bills, and grew closer. They married last year.

Leslie says that taking account of her spending shored up another relationship—her relationship with herself. "I felt like a thief in my own house, sneaking around. Admitting the truth was the hardest thing I think I've done. For at least a month I wished I'd kept my mouth shut. That's not how I feel now. My spending was out of control, and writing it down meant I had to justify why I ordered that two-hundred-dollar ring from the shopping channel. Recording what I spend keeps me honest."

Are you keeping money secrets from a spouse? Perhaps after you have worked your way through this book and feel financially literate, you'll open up to your loved one. Any mistakes you might have made in the past are just that, in the past. Whether you're working alone or in tandem, start tracking your expenditures.

TIPS FOR TRACKING YOUR EXPENDITURES

- **Collect receipts.** Store them in an unused wallet, purse, or in an envelope. Once a week, sort them into one of the three receipt files you have set up.

- **Record spending.** As soon as possible, record the amount you've spent in a small notebook, so the receipts don't pile up.

- **Remember noncash payments.** When you pay by check or credit card, you're still spending money, so record those expenditures, too.

- **Break down the costs.** As you work through this book, record your expenditures weekly for the next month. You can use the worksheets included at the end of this book.

If you can afford it, consider buying personal-finance software from companies such as Quicken, available at office-supply stores and online, to help you track your spending. And for a higher fee, the Web-based Mvelopes can help you keep track of your money down to the last dime. This service offers a thirty-day free trial from time to time and can be found online at www.mvelopes.com.

When you look at the results of your tracking, are there any surprises for you? Once you develop the habit of tracking your money, you won't have to wonder where it goes.

Next, record your income.

INCOME

Yours	
Your spouse's	
Alimony/child support	
Real estate	
Business	
Total	

Finally, subtract what you spend from the amount you have coming in.

Incoming	_____
−	
Outgoing	_____
Cash flow	_____

This difference between what you're spending and your income is your cash flow. If there's a hefty surplus, you're moving in the right direction. If there's only a small margin or a negative amount, there are ways to change your bottom line. That's where we're going to pick up in the next step.

HELPFUL HINT

If your spending pattern worries you, curbing ATM withdrawals can be helpful. Getting cash from these machines is so easy we often fail to make the connection with the hard work that went into earning it. If it's safe for you to carry money, do what Grandma Chips used to do and use envelopes. If you have $50 for eating out, put that money in an envelope and promise yourself that you won't spend another dime. To develop respect for your money, arrange bills in your wallet neatly and according to denomination; that way you won't be pulling out crumpled bills.

BUILDING FINANCIAL LITERACY

Many clients tell me that they want nothing to do with stocks. I don't believe in pushing clients in any direction, but I explain that they're probably already invested in the stock market, through their retirement plans. Some stocks tend to be volatile and others less risky. *Stock* is a share in the ownership of a company. The more stock you acquire, the greater your ownership stake. You'll learn much more about stocks later in this book.

"Know well the condition of your flocks, and give attention to your herds." Proverbs 27:23.

If the spirit moves you, read this passage aloud and write about its meaning as you become more financially literate.

_____

_____

_____

_____

_____

_____

_____

_____

STEP 4

Quit Strumming the Money Blues

7

Paying Down Debt

As you move toward your retirement goals, you might be worried about your debts. Maybe you hate to open the mail because you can't stand to look at high credit card or loan balances, or you're afraid to answer the phone because a collection agency might be calling to hound you. If that's the case, I hope you aren't thinking of yourself as stupid. By now you must know that intelligence, education, and professional status offer no protection against indebtedness.

In his memoir, *My Grandfather's Son*, Yale Law School graduate and Supreme Court justice Clarence Thomas tells of a humiliating experience that grew out of his inability to manage his personal finances. Before he was appointed as one of the nation's highest-ranking jurists, he served as the director of the U.S. Equal Employment Opportunity Commission. He was trying to rent a car, and the clerk called the credit card company for confirmation, then cut up his credit card on the spot. Justice Thomas's experience is not unique to any particular race. Americans have run up non-mortgage debts to the tune of $2.4 trillion. Debts don't only cause humiliation; they can destroy dreams and derail lives.

Divorce derailed television anchor Valerie Coleman Morris's retirement plans and catapulted her into debt. Valerie Coleman Morris *is* her real name. Unlike others introduced in this book, she's not one of my clients whose name and biographical details have been changed. The Emmy Award–winning anchorwoman is sharing her story as part of her commitment to teach financial literacy to women, young adults, and people of color, whom she describes as "the most disenfranchised segments of the population concerning money issues."

In a career spanning more than thirty years, Ms. Coleman Morris's face and jewel-toned voice grew familiar to nightly news viewers at stations in San Francisco, Los Angeles, and Manhattan, and her audience expanded when she became business anchor for the cable giant CNN, broadcasting throughout the United States and around the world.

Watching her, few people would have guessed that this exquisitely dressed, highly paid professional owed more than a million dollars, which included an unsold empty house in San Francisco and credit card and bank loan balances. Her eighteen-year marriage ended in California, a community-property state, which means that all property acquired, debts incurred, and income earned during a marriage and while a couple live together are split fifty/fifty if a union is dissolved. Ms. Coleman Morris was the major breadwinner. She says she was like many high-earning women who unconditionally share everything with lower-earning spouses.

When the marriage ended and she began receiving bills in both their names, she was shocked to learn that she was fully responsible for a $60,000 unpaid bank loan. She could have let the bills go unpaid, but that would have meant destroying her own credit rating. She says, "I could get mad or get even. I wasn't going to live my life as a pissed-off black woman. Debt is an awful situation, but it doesn't have to mean that your financial life is over. So I got even. And by that, I'm not speaking of retaliation. I wanted to get myself back on an even plane, restore the financial balance in my life." She was talking about getting into the black.

That wouldn't be easy, even for someone earning a high-six-figure salary. For years she lived below her means, developed a plan for paying down her debt, tracked her spending, saved what she could for retirement, and spent little on herself. Hardest of all for her, she stopped taking vacations. Fortunately, her job as a CNN financial anchor required her to develop an expertise in personal and high finances. In this manner, she took control of her life.

When the divorce was final and she'd paid off much of the debt, she booked her first recreational trip as a single woman. She bought a first-class ticket to Switzerland, where she attended the famed Montreux Jazz Festival. She was getting off the elevator at a luxury hotel when a handsome and confident black American man was about to board. The two struck up a conversation. He turned out to be businessman Robert Morris. Years later, in 1993, she married him.

Love and passion aside, Ms. Coleman Morris is quick to point out that she approached her second marriage in a radically different manner from the first, talking openly about money and who would bear responsibility for what. "I often tell couples about to wed that they should spend as much time talking about finances as they do making plans for their wedding. If you're planning to wed, find out whether your intended is a spender or a saver, and whether he or she is in debt. If so, discuss how you can deal with this."

She also advises couples to open three separate checking accounts: one for each individual and a joint account for paying bills. "You may be in love and want to be together, but your money doesn't have to cohabitate." Ms. Coleman Morris adds, "Everyone needs to have a separate financial identity. That means having some money of your own that you can spend without accounting to anyone else. It used to be called 'mad money,' and the amount is determined by income. Maybe you put aside a hundred dollars a month or fifty. This way you won't have to rely on a credit card for unanticipated expenses. And if something happens to his job or yours, the other still has a good financial foundation upon which the family can rely."

After taking some of her own advice about money, at the age of sixty Ms. Coleman Morris was able to decline a new CNN contract offer and retire from the company. She started a new career as a financial-literacy specialist. She continues to write and narrate the nationally syndicated radio column that she created in 1986, "With the Family in Mind," focusing on family issues and money matters, airing on CBS Radio Network three times a week.

In 2007 she and Mr. Morris moved to a new home in Arizona, from which she travels the country and the world teaching the gospel of financial literacy. She tells audiences that each dollar of paid-off debt has the potential to generate double-digit returns once it's freed up. She points out, for instance, that the $30,000 someone might pay in credit card interest over twelve years could be invested during a comparable period to grow into more than $100,000.[*]

Ms. Coleman Morris believes that one of the most important concepts to grasp concerns interest. "There's this saying: 'Those who understand compound interest earn it; those who don't will pay it.'" She's referring to the compound interest that accrues on credit card balances. She's not opposed to credit cards. "They aren't

---

[*] This figure is hypothetical and does not represent any particular investment. Positive results cannot be guaranteed when investing in equities. Investing involves risks, including possible loss of the principal.

bad. But there's a great deal of potential for abusing credit cards." While she points out that there are no quick fixes for repairing credit ratings, she has much to say about whittling away debt.

- **Write due dates on your calendar.** The single most important way to increase your credit rating is to pay your bills on time. That doesn't mean mailing off the check three days before it's due and crossing your fingers. Give the check time to be delivered, keeping in mind weekend office delays and time for your payment to be entered into the company's system. You might want to send the payment off about a week early. Even better, pay online so there's no delay or postage costs.

- **Negotiate for better interest rates.** If you're paying your credit card bills on time, call and ask for a supervisor and request a lower interest rate. If you don't get what you want, look for a company offering lower rates.

- **Don't pay just the minimum.** This usually doesn't cover the interest rate of what you owe. As the compound interest continues to build, you can get so far into debt with a company that you become a modern-day version of a sharecropper. If possible, pay the full amount and free yourself.

- **Pay off the card with the highest interest rate first.** If you owe more than one company, pay off the ones that are charging the most.

- **Read your credit reports.** After ordering your three free credit reports, go over them carefully. In a 2004 study by the U.S. Public Interest Research Group, 79 percent of credit reports contained errors; 25 percent contained errors that could mean getting denied a mortgage or turned down for a job. Humans are entering the data, so it's subject to error. Someone might have confused you with a person with a similar name who has an egregious payment profile, or a thief might have been using your information to obtain credit. There's information in the report that explains how to dispute an error and get it corrected.

What's up next for Ms. Coleman Morris? With her husband's help, she will take her financial-literacy messages on a tour of historically black colleges. She is also working on a financial book for young African Americans. She plans to interview black celebrities who will share their financial stories and offer tips on how to go "green," in hopes of improving tomorrow's financial climate. Valerie Coleman Morris can be contacted through her website, www.moneyval.net.

Before I close this subject of debt, I want to mention that not all loans come from banks and credit card companies. In my practice, I often hear complaints about loans made to family members and friends, debts that have not been repaid and therefore throw people off track in their retirement planning.

I always remind clients that if they are considering making a personal loan that they need to have repaid, it might be best to say no. If the friend or relative is asking you as a last resort, that means that no other institution is willing to trust this individual.

If the client decides to grant the loan, I advise asking the borrower to sign a promissory note that governs how the money will be repaid—in installment payments or a lump sum—and at what interest rate, if any. A promissory note protects the lender, and since it makes the loan more official, it can give the debtor a sense of dignity concerning the transaction. I have made a lot of loans, and I've found that those that included promissory notes, as opposed to "handshake" loans, tend to be repaid. An attorney can draw up one of these notes for you, or you can get one online from firms such as www.nolo.com and www.agreementsetc.com/loan-agreement. If you have defaulted on a loan from an individual, contact the person, pledge to repay the loan, and do it. Repaying is a matter of integrity, and it will not only make the person who lent you the money feel better, but this will also help you maintain a sense of self respect.

Finally, let me mention that several of my clients have been helped by reading *Zero Debt: The Ultimate Guide to Financial Freedom*, written by African American personal-finance expert Lynnette Khalfani.

If you're feeling desperately squeezed by debt, here are more strategies:

- **Make it a part-time affair.** Get an extra job, which might mean working in a department store, neighborhood shop, et cetera, for the purpose of paying down your debts. If working an extra job seems onerous, remind yourself that it's just temporary. Knowing that you're taking action might help you sleep better.

- **Recover from compulsive debting.** Debtors Anonymous offers no-cost recovery techniques and support based on principles of the AA 12-step groups. These groups meet in cities around the country. For more information, go online to www.debtorsanonymous.org or phone the main office in Needham, Massachusetts, at

(781) 453-2743. Also, read the excellent book based on Debtors Anonymous principles, *How to Get Out of Debt, Stay Out of Debt, and Live Prosperously* by Jerrold Mundis, and Glinda Bridgforth's financial guides, including *Girl! Get Your Credit Straight: A Sister's Guide to Ditching Your Debt, Mending Your Credit, and Building a Strong Financial Future.*

- **Sign up for the Financial Peace Program University.** Radio host Dave Ramsey's program is utilized by individuals, churches, corporations, and military units. Several program packages are available at a range of prices, but *The Dave Ramsey Show*, which has been on the radio for more than fifteen years, playing on hundreds of stations across the country, can be heard for free. You can locate the show on a station near you by going online to www.daveramsey.com or find him on Fox TV Business Network.

- **Consider a debt-management counselor.** If you turn to a nonprofit credit-counseling firm for help, your adviser may recommend a debt-management plan. This means that the firm will negotiate an agreement between you and your creditors and arrange to pay your debts with your money. Use of a debt-management plan will be noted on your credit report, but if you adhere to the agreement by making the consolidated payment on time each month, your credit score will recover eventually.

- **Consider bankruptcy as a last-ditch effort.** In this federal court proceeding, your assets are liquidated and you're relieved of further liability. Bankruptcy can deal a devastating blow to your credit score. It takes seven to ten years before the bankruptcy drops off your credit report.

- **Avoid "credit repair" companies.** The only way to truly fix your credit report is to pay your bills consistently over time. Companies that promise to repair your report for you should be regarded as scams.

- **If you're incarcerated and have unpaid child-support payments accruing, consider writing to the court that ordered you to pay to request that payments be suspended during your incarceration.** State that you will start paying after your release, and at that time make every effort to care for your child. Our children need emotional, physical, and financial support from both parents.

- **If you were incarcerated, use debt repayment to restore your name.** Ex-offenders often leave prison saddled with debts for child support, drunk-driving violations, and fees for anger management, drug treatment, and DNA and drug testing. Debts can compound the difficulty of starting a new life. But by repaying them, you can use financial records to show prospective employers and landlords that you are a person of integrity. It won't be easy. You might have to take jobs that few others want. But brick by brick, you can build self-respect and your credit score.

No matter your situation, if you're worried about debts, praying can help bring you peace of mind. Remember that credit card companies employ behavioral psychologists to figure out what kind of images and words can convince consumers to buy. They are waging a battle to make you part with your money. Pray for strength to resist these messages. I've provided space below for you to continue writing about what makes you most grateful. This will help you remember that much of what we value cannot be purchased with credit cards.

_____

_____

_____

HELPFUL HINT

List some relaxing, inexpensive activities to remind yourself that something like a good hearty laugh with a pal is worth millions. What comes to mind?

What I Can Enjoy for Free

○ _____

○ _____

○ _____

Here are a few ideas: Taking a long, invigorating walk with a loved one. Host (whether in a park or a table at the mall) a lunch that's prepared with food you already have at home. If Thanksgiving is approaching, collect fall leaves that you can dry and use as inexpensive table decorations. And don't forget sorting and organizing old photos, a few at a time, to bring back fond memories. If you're in the mood to laugh, rent a Tyler Perry film, and if you feel like shouting, listen to Nina Simone's recording of the song, "Freedom!"

BUILDING FINANCIAL LITERACY

If an individual borrows something and backs up the promise to repay by offering a car, boat, or house as collateral, that's *secured debt*. If the borrower defaults on the loan, the lender has the legal right to claim the property listed as collateral as full or partial payment. If a loan is granted on the basis of someone's promise to repay, without pledging property, this is *unsecured debt*. Most credit card debts are unsecured, while home loans are secured. The difference between the two types of loans explains why holding a lot of unsecured debt can affect your credit score negatively, and why higher interest is charged on what are considered riskier unsecured loans.

> **SECURED DEBT:**
> Debt that is backed up with collateral, giving the lender the right, in the event of default, to seize the asset

> **UNSECURED DEBT:**
> Debt that is not backed up with collateral

"He did what was right in the sight of the Lord, just as his ancestor David had done." —2 Chronicles 29:2.

If the spirit moves you, read this passage aloud and write about its meaning as you become more financially literate.

_____

_____

_____

_____

_____

_____

_____

_____

_____

8

Maximizing Your Cash

Eddie and I attended Richmond's Jefferson-Huguenot-Wythe High School together. I played football while he ran track. Neither of us came from families that could afford to send us to college, but both of us were determined to get ahead. Football was my ticket to the University of Richmond, while Eddie chose the military, enrolling after graduation and later using the GI benefits to pay for his college degree.

Fast-forward to the 1990s, when I told Eddie I was becoming a financial planner. He signed on as one of my first clients. Both of us had married and started families of our own, and money was scarce. I often use Eddie's story when I speak to those who have little but who want to make the most of it as they move toward retirement.

As a career military man, Eddie had a relatively low salary, but he knew how to maximize his cash. When some of the other service personnel invited him to join them at bars, Eddie said no, that he needed to hang on to what he had. He and his wife had purchased a house in Washington, D.C., and at first they only had $50 a month to set aside. On my advice, they invested that in mutual funds, eventually increasing the amount to $100 and then $200 and $300 a month. And they kept making the most of what they had, taking whatever money they earned in raises and socking it into their retirement accounts, cutting back on spending wherever possible. Today Eddie is only a few years away from retirement. We were together the other day, reviewing his financial-worth statement. Eddie is now worth $1.3 million, and that doesn't include the pension he'll receive. He has come a long way from our dog days of high school.

What about you? What's in your future? If you're feeling wrung out from tracking what you spend and paying down your debts, this step might allow you to catch your breath. It's designed to elicit the kind of emotions you might experience if you pulled into a lookout point along a highway. You already know that you have a way to go before reaching your destination, but you've made substantial progress. Taking a detour is out of the question, but taking a breath is not and you pull over. I'm not talking about a quick stop at one of those rest areas with grubby bathrooms and overpriced fast food; I mean pausing along a ridge at a spot that affords an exceptional view. You climb out and lean on your car, perhaps feeling the engine's warmth, as you consider the life that stretches before you. All the while traffic whizzes by, as it should, since life, with its demands and complicated realities, never stands still. But you can pause because in racing ahead you might miss opportunities to maximize the cash you already have by changing old patterns and creating new ones.

I think I hear someone shouting, "I don't have cash to maximize!" If that's what you're thinking, I hope to prove you wrong. As a man of faith, I believe that our world is filled with abundance.

And as the grandson of a domestic worker and a butcher who raised six children, I have seen how a little bit can be stretched into plenty. How do we do this with money? Let me count the ways:

1. Find out what you're earning on savings and checking accounts. Banks earn the bulk of their money by lending out a percentage of their deposits for mortgages, car loans, et cetera, and by charging substantially higher interest than they pay their depositors. There's nothing wrong with that. Banks are businesses, which means they're supposed to make money. But it's your business to get into the black, and that means you're supposed to make money, too. If you don't know how much interest you're getting paid for your savings and checking accounts, look over your bank documents or ask a bank manager. Compare that figure with current prevailing interest rates by going online to www.bankrate.com. This website, which bills itself as offering "comprehensive, objective and free" information, is updated daily. Click the "Savings and Checking" tab, and you'll see a highlighted box that lists national savings and checking interest rates. If you discover that you're being underpaid, this relatively minor difference says something about how you do business. You should put your money where it's treated well.

2. Check out CD rates. If you want to continue doing business with your bank, consider moving some of your money to a certificate of deposit (CD). These offer higher rates of return but tie up your money for a specified period of three months to five years. By investing in a CD you are locking in an interest rate, which will remain the same whether

rates go up or down. Money removed before maturity is subject to a penalty. For those who might be tempted to spend unnecessarily, having money tied up and out of reach may keep you from dipping into your savings. CD rates vary from bank to bank. For information on the best offers available, go online to www.bankrate.com.

3. Get a raise from a money market account. MMAs offer about twice the interest of traditional savings accounts. You can write checks on these accounts, and MMAs are available through most banks or credit unions. The drawback is that there is often a higher minimum balance required than for opening a savings account, but these amounts vary among institutions.

4. Bank online. Online banks don't have to pay the same overhead costs as brick-and-mortar institutions, so they can offer higher interest rates to depositors. Many people only feel safe putting their money into brick-and-mortar banks. They don't trust online checking or savings accounts because they can't walk into the place. They fear that virtual banks will shut down overnight, leaving them broke and feeling foolish. If that kind of fear is holding you back, you might find it comforting to choose an online bank that is connected to a long-established institution.

5. Use preventive care. Keep a checking account rather than paying for money orders, which if lost won't be reimbursed for months. Steer clear of ATMs that charge you fees for transactions. Keep your checking account balanced so you don't wind up paying overdraft fees. Open accounts with

established banks that offer a bonus deposit, such as $25 or $50, when you join.

6. **Stop overpaying Uncle Sam.** It's understandable that folks like getting a big refund each spring. They know they're overpaying in taxes, but it's almost as if they're being forced to save. Voluntary losing is more like it. Those extra dollars could be maximized in a high-interest account. You absolutely want to pay Uncle Sam, but not more than he's due. If you work for someone else, consistently receive hundreds of dollars in annual refunds, and your income has not risen significantly, you may want to seek out a professional for advice on how much you should be paying. If you cut back on what you're paying the government, be sure to save or invest the amount you've been overpaying. If you're self-employed, keep up on your quarterly tax payments, so you don't wind up paying a penalty. If you need help to adjust your withholding, use the *Kiplinger's* online refund calculator at www.kiplingerforecast.com/tools.

7. **Use flexible-spending accounts.** FSAs are benefits that some companies offer to help pay for child care, elder care, and health care. Here's how they work: An employee designates an amount to spend in the coming year on health care (including copays and prescriptions), dental care, child care, and elder care. That amount is deducted, pretax, from payroll. The employee is reimbursed after a bill is submitted to the flexible-spending insurer. The advantage of FSAs is that they save on taxes. The disadvantage is that the employee might overestimate how much is

needed or fail to apply for reimbursement, losing out on that money. Before signing up, it can help to track your expenditures.

> **FLEXIBLE-SPENDING ACCOUNT:**
> Account in which employee pretax dollars can be spent on health care, child care, or elder care

8. Avoid expensive out-of-pocket health-care fees. Sure, it's a pain to struggle through the voice-mail maze if you're trying to find out whether the doctor, therapist, dentist, or lab that you want to use is on the approved list. But even if you aren't required to get preauthorization from a primary-care physician to see a specialist, such as a dermatologist, call before you visit a new doctor, lab, or clinic, or if you're visiting someone you've used before, or after changing insurance companies. This gives you a measure of control in a system that forces clients to wait for weeks or months to get a refund or to learn that the claim was denied or the amount reduced. Health-care providers train their employees to deny clients as often as possible. By calling ahead, you can at least find out whether you've met the deductible or whether the care you're seeking will be considered for reimbursement. So making that frustrating phone call can save you big-time.

9. Reconsider penny-pinchers. There's a high intolerance level in our community for people we label as "cheap." Think of the women you might know who refuse to date

men who "buy their suits at Sears" and of the almost universal derision about men or women who drive old cars. The message is that we should only drive or wear that which is most costly, even at the risk of financial impoverishment. We need to rethink these attitudes, which can lead us to spend rather than save, showboat rather than invest to maximize what we have. One of the gifts that can emerge from our struggles or worries about money is a renewed respect for those who are thrifty.

Before leaving your lookout point, take in the view one more time. As we develop financial literacy, the clouds that once obscured our vision begin to dissipate. We are reminded in the creation story that God is a generous God and His gifts continue to unfold. How should we translate that message in our materialistic, consumerist society?

I can tell you how one of the world's richest women, Zhang Yin of China, acted on the belief that one man's garbage might be another's jewels. Only a few years ago, she and her husband were in the United States driving around in an old Dodge minivan, scouring garbage dumps for scrap paper. She exported the scrap back to China—where paper was invented sometime around 100 B.C. and where there is now a paper shortage—and had it recycled to make corrugated cardboard boxes. Zhang Yin has made a fortune that is now estimated at over $1.5 billion—because she saw what others did not.

It's not necessary to go to China to be reminded that we live on fertile ground. College student Corey Kossack of Arizona, the son of a financial adviser, grew up hearing his dad talk about the importance of maximizing resources, and he took the idea seriously. He was a sophomore at Arizona State, trolling the eBay website, when he noticed that lots of folks were trying to unload their used DVDs. He got the idea of buying the old DVDs from individuals and reselling them in bulk. With $1,000 from his savings, he started his own company. Two years later, he'd sold half a million DVDs and was on his way to becoming a millionaire.

Corey Kossack and Zhang Yin reclaimed the old and made it new. Getting into the black may require changing the way you relate to this world. As you move on to the next task, determining how much you will need to last the rest of your life, it can be comforting to remember that your journey can be accomplished with small steps.

HELPFUL HINT

If you have a traditional pension plan, phone your human resources department or benefits administrator, explain your target date for retirement, and request a written estimate of how much you will receive each month after you retire. That statement will include, if you are married, a calculation of what your spouse will receive in the event of your death. While you have that representative on the phone, ask questions and take notes concerning additional benefits, such as life insurance, health care, moving expenses, et cetera. Be sure to ask for the representative's name and direct number so you can include this information in your file. Ask how long it will take to get the written estimate, pencil in that date on your calendar, and if you haven't heard from the company two weeks after that date, call again and inquire about the delay.

BUILDING FINANCIAL LITERACY

If you are planning to return to college, perhaps to earn a graduate degree, you may be eligible for a *tax credit*. People sometimes confuse these with tax deductions, but tax credits are far better, since the amount allowed is deducted from what's owed at the end of the

1040 form, reducing a tax bill dollar for dollar. What else qualifies for a tax credit? In addition to the Hope tax credit, which applies to tuition and related expenses for first- and second-year college students, there is the lifetime learning credit, for money spent on qualified tuition payments for postsecondary education. A retirement savings contribution tax credit allows those with even modest incomes to get tax credits of 10 to 50 percent of the amount contributed to a 401(k)-type plan or individual retirement account. To learn more, call the IRS Information Help Line at (800) 824-1040, or ask your tax preparer.

TAX CREDIT:
Directly reduces the amount of income tax that's owed, dollar for dollar

CONSIDERING SCRIPTURE

"Whoever is faithful in a very little is faithful also in much; and whoever is dishonest in a very little is dishonest also in much." —Luke 16:10.
If the spirit moves you, read this passage aloud and write about its meaning as you become more financially literate.

9

Pinpointing the Amount
You Need to Retire

You have geared up for this work by setting goals, paying yourself, tracking your spending, and confronting your debts. In the previous chapter you were asked to imagine driving on a highway and then pulling over to a lookout point to pause and consider how to maximize your money. Now that your thoughts are clarified, it's time to rev your engine and pick up speed in shaping your financial future.

Here in this chapter, the rubber meets the road. This is the heart of financial planning, when clients calculate how much they need to fund their goals, which often include retiring and remaining in the black. This is one of the most dynamic aspects of the process. Clients become true believers as they recognize that financial literacy makes them like the Little Engine That Could, empowering them to get where they want to go.

It doesn't always start out feeling exhilarating, however. Many of my clients get to this point and cannot imagine ever having enough money to reach their goals. During our second meeting, Shirley and Abdul Jackson were feeling anxious. "I've been awake all night," the forty-one-year-old Mrs. Jackson said. Her husband, also forty-one, said that he, too, had tossed and turned. Their discomfort was heightened by the memory of warnings from Mrs. Jackson's parents that if the couple wed, they would "start out broke, make less than nothing, and wind up in the streets."

Mrs. Jackson, the adopted daughter of a surgeon, had been raised in luxury in one of Virginia's wealthiest black families. Much to her parents' disappointment, after graduating from a private high school she ruled out college and instead burned through a small inheritance while living in a Rasta commune in Jamaica, West Indies. Fifteen years later, upon her return to the States, she got a job at a correctional institution. That was where she met Mr. Jackson, who at the time was an inmate.

Raised in a Richmond housing project, Mr. Jackson was the son of a convict. I won't share his biographical details, for they are distressingly familiar. In general, however, I can tell you that he is the product of America's so-called black underclass, which is viewed by the larger society with fear, hatred, and contempt. He is one of millions whose options are limited by racism, substandard education, and lack of job opportunities.

What we almost never see on the front pages or the nightly news reports are the thousands of untold stories of black-underclass achievements, of people who grew up neglected and abused and yet managed to beat the odds and create better lives. But poverty and oppression do take a toll, leading many to exist in quiet despair, while others resort to crime and rage-fueled self-destructive behaviors.

As a result, although African Americans are only 13 percent of the nation's population, half of this country's prison inmates are black. I don't excuse those who break the law, and yet it's no secret that our justice system deals out harsher penalties to African Americans. According to Harvard University's Dr. Orlando Patterson, one third of black men in their thirties have prison records.

At the age of twenty, Mr. Jackson was convicted for possession of drugs, and he served eight years in prison. After he was released and married, he and his wife learned a harsh lesson. Once prisoners are released, those in the larger society make them feel further disenfranchised by treating them with hostility and disapproval. Mrs. Jackson's parents were opposed to the marriage, and after severing ties with the couple they later refused to meet their twin grandsons, who were six years old when I began working with the couple.

Mr. Jackson had contacted me, voicing frustration, after he'd spent $11,000—he and his wife's entire savings—to pay off credit card debts that his wife had incurred by charging dental bills, designer clothing and accessories for their children, a luxury purse for herself, and hair weaving. He worried that her spending would keep them from ever saving anything for retirement. She later said that she initially resisted coming in because she didn't think they earned enough to work with a financial adviser. This is a mistake people make all the time, putting off financial planning because they want to wait until they "get their money straight." They don't realize that financial know-how can help them expedite that goal.

Mr. Jackson had developed an interest in personal finance years earlier. He worked at a local supermarket, and during one of my shopping trips, the two of us struck up a series of conversations. He knew that prisoners often had children who became prisoners and was determined that his newborn sons wouldn't follow in his footsteps, as he had in his father's. I had tremendous respect for him. The fact that he had a job made him unique. A 2005 study by two Princeton University sociology professors found that white males with criminal records were just as likely as blacks with no criminal records to find jobs. You can imagine how much harder it is for a black man with a record to get hired.

When I was leaving the credit union to open my own practice, Mr. Jackson predicted that he would become one of my first clients. We didn't keep in touch, but three years later, in 1996, I felt a tremendous sense of responsibility and gratitude as I helped him and his wife figure out "their price"—the amount that suggests how much they would need to meet their two most important goals: providing for their sons' college education and saving enough for retirement.

Mrs. Jackson was still employed at the federal correctional institution, although she had cut back her hours after the birth of their sons. She took home $835 a month. Mr. Jackson's supermarket work netted $947 a month. After four weeks of tracking expenditures, they found that their $1,782-a-month income was divvied up as follows:

$400—rent
$300—food
$150—tithe
$150—gas, tolls, loan payments, and insurance for a 1992 station wagon
$120—health insurance
$115—miscellaneous
$95—utilities
$50—savings
$1,380—total

Income: $1,782
Minus expenses: −$1,380
                     $ 402

Before her marriage, an aunt had left Mrs. Jackson $10,000, but this and more had been wiped out when they paid off their credit cards. You can see by their list of expenses that they lived beneath their means, which is why they had a surplus of $402 a month. But much of that surplus was accounted for. In considering their goals, they had listed "helping our sons attend college" as a top priority. If all went according to plan, their boys would enter their freshman year in 2008.

Their parents had set a goal that was attainable because they were planning ahead. With twelve years to save, the Jacksons figured out the specifics of what they could afford. Armed with information, they worked out a plan. If their sons chose to do so, they could live at home while attending a local public college. Mrs. Jackson researched tuition costs at several schools, and she and her husband followed a path chosen by a growing number of parents.

They set up a 529 prepaid college plan with the state of Virginia. These plans are offered in every state and are available up to five years before a student starts college. With college costs rising at twice the rate of inflation, the greatest benefit of the prepaid plan is that it freezes prices. Here's what I mean: In 1996, when I began working with the Jacksons, a four-year education at a state college cost $15,215. The Jacksons doubled that sum to $32,430, to provide for both their children.

This sounded costly to the Jacksons because they weren't fully taking into account the impact of inflation. By 2008, that same undergraduate education would cost $48,000 for both their sons, rather than $32,430—nearly a $16,000 difference. As Mrs. Jackson pointed out, using a prepaid plan is like putting an item on layaway, paying for it a bit at a time. With twelve years to go, and twelve months in each year, they would make a total of 144 monthly payments at $318 a month. This was a sum they could handle. Excited by the prospect of providing for their sons' college costs, they had applied for the prepaid tuition plan and were waiting for the paperwork to arrive. The only problem was that it would wipe out all but $84 of their $402 surplus.

"We won't have much left for emergencies," Mrs. Jackson said with a frown. "How will we ever pay for retirement?"

I responded by teaching them a simple rule of thumb, which you might find helpful later in this chapter, when you project how much you will want for your retirement. The initial calculation should be based on what you're spending now. I told the Jacksons, "Look over your expenses. How much do you *need* for living in today's dollars?"

Mr. Jackson ran a finger down his cash-flow statement and gave me a bemused look, as if I'd asked a trick question." It says we need seventeen hundred dollars a month."

"And then there's nothing left for gifts, eating out, nothing," Mrs. Jackson added.

"That's right," I said, encouraging her. "You like buying little extras for your sons, and you want to have money saved for emergencies and entertainment. That sounds reasonable. You just told me what you *need*. How much do you *want* in today's dollars?"

Mrs. Jackson turned to her husband. "We don't want anything fancy. We just want to have enough. Two thousand a month would be perfect, but how can we—"

"Hold on, please," I said. "Let's go with that figure." I wrote it down and showed it to them. You *want* two thousand a month in today's dollars."

In our initial work together they had honed in on a retirement date. They were both forty-one and hoped to retire at sixty-two on June 1, 2017. They had also worked through the uncomfortable process of coming up with a mortality date, in other words, the estimation of their age at death. They were in good physical condition, and God willing, health insurance would help them remain that way. They'd estimated that they would live until age ninety. That meant they would have twenty-eight years of retirement.

I explained why I had been repeating the phrase "in today's dollars." The amount they wanted for living comfortably in the present would be enough to retire on, but only if they retired immediately. Inflation has been rising at a rate of about 3 percent each year since 1987. I showed them an inflation table (included on page 130) that would help them calculate how much they would need when they retire in 2017. As you've learned, inflation is part of life. You can't mail a letter today for the price you paid ten years ago, and sending a letter will cost more ten years from now than it does today. My goal in planning for the Jackons' retirement was to give them the same buying power in the future that they had in the present with $2,000. The new inflation-adjusted figure came to $3,721, almost double.

People are often shocked at inflation-adjusted figures. I remember my great-aunt Wa-Wa saying that her Social Security check seemed to buy half of what it once did, and she was right. When she retired from domestic work in her sixties, her check seemed like enough to make her life comfortable. Ten years later, that was hardly the case.

We don't tend to notice the effects of inflation because prices increase in small increments. But when we're planning for retirement and look down the road at what lies ahead, inflation can be shocking. The blessing is that once we have an inkling of what to expect, we can prepare by planning. That was just what the Jacksons were doing, despite their anxieties.

One note about their calculations: It was true that the Jacksons' expenses would decrease as their children finished college and moved away from home. And after retirement, the couple wouldn't be paying Social Security taxes. But since no one but God knows what lies ahead, it's always advantageous to base figures on how much we want for a comfortable life in the here and now.

The Jacksons were aiming for $3,721 a month. I multiplied that by 12 for the months of the year and came up with $44,652 annually. That was more than twice what they earned.

Hearing the sum aloud, Mrs. Jackson stood, holding her stomach. In a soothing voice, her husband asked her to remain quiet while I finished. He might have been bracing himself to hear the far more substantial figure that was coming. I was calculating $44,652 times 28, the number of years they hoped to live in retirement. The room was so quiet that we could have heard a pin drop. I said, "You'll need $1,250,256."

Mrs. Jackson began crying. "This is like a bad joke."

Her husband held her in his arms, talking to her while looking over her shoulder and holding my gaze. "Sugar, you always say I'm good at readin' people. Aaron ain't playin' us. He thinks we can pull this off. Let's give him time to finish."

I laid their financial documents across my desk and, one at a time, pointed to the bottom lines. Mrs. Jackson was working part-time but had once been a full-time employee. "According to these pension calculations, you'll receive eight hundred dollars a month income for the rest of your life." I multiplied that amount by 28, repeating the calculations aloud: "That's $800 times twelve months, which is $9,600 a year. If you receive that amount for twenty-eight years, it adds up to $268,800."

"You mean we can—" Mrs. Jackson interrupted herself.

I directed their gaze to her Social Security statement. "At the minimum, your benefits will be $1,100 a month. Over a period of twenty-eight years, that comes to $369,600."

They had caught on by now, and Mr. Jackson reached for his own Social Security statement. "You've told me that Social Security will still be around in the future, even though it's gotta change. It says here that I'll be paid $937 a month." He turned the calculator around and did the math. "That's $314,832."

I said, "Your three income sources total $953,232. You will need $297,024 over the next twenty-one years to make up the difference. With investments, and an eight percent growth* over twenty-one years, that will work out to"—my fingers were moving quickly, punching in digits—"$471 a month."

I heard Mr. Jackson exhale. He snapped his fingers to indicate that it seemed doable. "I can find a second job, save that and for day-to-day extras."

"No, you already work too hard," Mrs. Jackson said. "The boys need you."

"We'll figure it out," he assured her. I knew they would. If he couldn't get another job, they could always decide to delay their retirement.

Mr. Jackson thanked me. "You even had *me* worried there for a while."

He and his wife were smiling at each other. I never get enough of these moments, seeing looks of relief as people taste for the first time the promise of a comfortable future. I'll return to the Jacksons at chapter's end, but first it's time for you to determine your retirement numbers.

To start, you'll want to grab several sheets of paper or your journal, a calculator, and your cash-flow statement and retirement documents. The calculation process works the same, no matter the amount of your combined goals. The following instructions will help you fill out the Funding Chart (see page 130).

---

* This figure is hypothetical and does not represent any particular investment product. Positive results are not guaranteed when investing in equities. Investing involves risk, including possible loss of principal.

Funding Your Retirement

1. Look over your cash-flow statement to discern how much income you *need* annually in today's dollars, and record that amount on the Funding Chart. How much do you *want* annually to live comfortably in today's dollars? Record that amount. Divide the amount you want by 12, and record that figure.

2. Fill in the date you plan to retire and what your age will be. Figure out how many years you have until you retire by subtracting the current year from your retirement year. For instance, if it's 2009 and you plan to retire in 2019, you have ten years. Record the years and months on the Funding Chart.

3. Estimate your mortality age, adding an extra five years for peace of mind, and record that age on the chart. Now calculate the number of years you expect to live in retirement by subtracting your retirement age from your mortality age, and record that number. If you plan to retire in 2020, at seventy-two, and you expect to live until you're one hundred, you would have twenty-eight years in retirement.

4. Take the amount you *want* and adjust for inflation by consulting the Inflation-Factor Table (see page 130). It's always helpful to stay apprised of changing economic trends, and you can do this by using online sites such as www.infla tiondata.com (on the left-hand side go to "Inflation" and then "Current Inflation"). For now, you may be able to adjust for inflation using 3 percent, the average historical rate. You'll

notice that the Inflation-Factor Table indicates changes in increments of five years. If you're retiring in less than five years or just over ten, choose the closest number. The numbers, such as 1.16 or 1.34, are factors, mathematical formulas that help break down complex numbers.

5. Multiply the factor closest to the number of years until you retire by the amount of money you want for retirement. For instance, if you wanted $1,000 a month in today's dollars and you are going to retire in ten years, you would multiply 1,000 times 1.34. Your answer would be $1,340 a month. Fill in your inflation-adjusted monthly cost on the Funding Chart.

6. Multiply the monthly inflation-adjusted sum by the twelve months of the year. For instance, $1,340 × 12 = $16,080 annually.

7. Multiply this inflation-adjusted yearly amount by the number of years you expect to live in retirement. For instance, if you expect to live for thirty years in retirement and want to have $16,080 a year, you would need $482,400 during retirement. Fill in your amount under "my price."

8. Compute how much money you will receive from various sources. If you will get Social Security, look at the amount you are scheduled to receive at your chosen retirement age. Multiply that amount times the number of years you will live in retirement. If you'll live in retirement for twenty years and will receive $1,000 a month, you would multiply the monthly sum by 12. In this case, that would come to $12,000 a year. Multiply that annual sum by the number of

years you expect to live in retirement. Fill in those amounts under "My income sources."

9. Calculate other sources of monthly income, using the directions described above. Mrs. Jackson works for the federal government and was offered a pension through her job. Fewer jobs offer that valuable option these days. But as you will see in coming chapters, individuals can purchase pension-like plans of their own.

10. Add the various sums of all your income sources. Write this amount under "My total income."

11. Subtract this amount from "my price." For instance, if your price is $600,00, and you have $550,000 covered, the difference would be $50,000. If you have a surplus, you can figure out later whether this will be sufficient for funding your other goals. If you will not have enough from your income sources, please read the next instruction at the bottom of this page.

12. Divide whatever sum is left over by the number of years you have until retirement. Record that amount under "I need $ _____," and fill in the time you have before retirement. For instance, if you have eight years until retirement and $40,000 that you need to make up, you know you will need to generate $5,000 a year in retirement savings.

Should you find that you don't have enough time to generate your retirement fund, you may want to consider working longer, accelerating your savings so you can catch up, or generating more cash through one of the many solutions that will be offered in step 5.

INFLATION-FACTOR TABLE

Number of years until retirement	5	10	15	20	25
Inflation factor: 3%	1.16	1.34	1.56	1.81	2.09
Inflation factor: 4%	1.22	1.48	1.80	2.19	2.67

Funding Chart

○ How much I need $ _____

○ How much I want $ _____

○ I want $ _____ per month

○ I will retire (month) _____, (year) 20 __ at age _____

○ I have _____ years until retirement

○ My estimated mortality age is _____

○ I will have _____ years in retirement

○ The amount I want monthly in today's dollars is
$ _____ × 12 months = $ _____ × inflation factor _____ = (inflation-adjusted sum) $ _____

○ (Inflation-adjusted sum) $ _____ × _____ years in retirement = $ _____ : my price

○ My income sources:

- Social Security: $ _____ × 12 months × _____ years in retirement = $ _____
- Pension $ _____ × 12 months × _____ years in retirement = $ _____
- _____ (other sources) × 12 months × _____ years in retirement = $ _____
- My total income $ _____
- − $ _____ (my price)
- I have $ _____ (surplus)
- I have $ _____ (deficit). Continue if you have a deficit.
- I need $ _____
- I have _____ years to raise $ _____

Whatever your result, remind yourself that you've just accomplished what millions of others have not. You have figured out what you need, and that means you're several steps ahead of where you were when you started this work.

There is no way to predict whether your life will follow the route you are charting. The Jacksons, for instance, experienced some disappointments. Mr. Jackson lost his supermarket job, and unable to secure another, he started a small business. He used computer graphics to impose quotations from black leaders over photographs his wife had taken in Jamaica and offered them for sale. They continue to sell briskly, and he has kept up with his Social Security payments. His compensation has increased from what they were expecting. When their sons were in fifth grade, Mrs. Jackson returned to full-time work, which increased her pension.

The family also experienced a crisis. One of their twin sons was riding in a car with a boy who held up a convenience store, and both young men were arrested at the scene of the crime. I learned of this when Mr. Jackson called to ask about recommendations for an attorney. His voice quavered as he told me of the incident, and he added that his in-laws had heard of their troubles and offered to help. Mr. Jackson turned them down, insisting that he could pay the legal tab on his own. He was right; he could afford to. After a long and grueling ordeal, both their sons entered college in 2008, as their parents had hoped they would.

What are your dreams? And how will you cushion yourself so that you're prepared for the vicissitudes of the future? In step 5, you will learn of various strategies designed to make up for any short-falls you might face.

HELPFUL HINT

Millions of people die without drawing up a will, in which case the courts appoint representatives to distribute the deceased person's assets. You'll want to create a will to address who will inherit from you and other issues. You can consult an attorney or get a simple, low-cost will drawn up through one of the online services. You might also consider putting together a list of your secret passwords on your accounts and your account numbers for the executor of your estate to minimize confusion after your death.

BUILDING FINANCIAL LITERACY

A lot of people hear the term *tax shelter* and picture rich fat cats wiring millions to the islands in an illegal attempt to avoid paying Uncle Sam. But the term simply refers to methods of reducing taxable income so you owe the government less.

There are many legal tax shelters. We've discussed tax-deferred 529 college savings accounts, prepaid tuition plans, and retirement savings accounts—all of which are tax shelters. They allow you to pay out less to the state and federal governments, giving you more opportunities to get into the black.

CONSIDERING SCRIPTURE

"For which of you, intending to build a tower, does not first sit down and estimate the cost, to see whether he has enough to complete it?" —Luke 14:28.

If the spirit moves you, read this passage aloud and write about its meaning as you become more financially literate.

_____

_____

_____

_____

_____

_____

STEP 5

Put the Pieces Together

10

Knowing When to Take Social Security

In fifteen years of practice, I've seen the pendulum swing in client attitudes about Social Security retirement-income benefits. During the mid–1990s, many of my older clients seemed in awe of the checks they were scheduled to receive. They were counting on Social Security to cover their needs, from retirement until the day they died.

This attitude was a response to events that transpired long before I was born. In the 1940s, when the government started sending monthly payments to the elderly, many African Americans had reason to believe that they would never get Social Security checks when they grew too old to work. They had been shut out of Social Security by powerful legislators who excluded domestic and agricultural occupations from this new government benefit, out of fear of losing their grip on their labor force. These legislators wanted to preserve the Southern Way of Life, with fields tended by low-wage workers and white-owned homes cleaned, laundry washed, and food prepared by domestics who often worked until they were seventy-five.

According to Ira Katznelson, Columbia University professor of political science and history, some White House advisers wanted old-age insurance to be more inclusive, but southern politicians prevailed. By the time President Franklin D. Roosevelt signed the 1935 Social Security Act, it was worded deliberately to deny benefits to people employed as maids and agricultural workers. At the time, this represented half the workers in the United States and more than 60 percent of African Americans.

This exclusion was eliminated in 1954, but even then, as Dr. Katznelson writes in *When Affirmative Action Was White*, "African Americans were not able to catch up, since the program required at least five years of contributions before benefits could be received." Despite changes to the Social Security laws, many domestics and agricultural laborers worked for private employers who didn't report their wages, so they were still unable to qualify for benefits. Some elderly clients that I later advised secured jobs in school cafeterias and factories or worked as domestics in offices, department stores, hospitals, and banks: Social Security–qualified jobs. Decades later, when they discussed their early losses, I didn't detect bitterness. They'd worked hard and earned little, but they were profoundly relieved to realize that they would be afforded some measure of financial protection in old age through Social Security. I often heard them say, "I just need a little bit to get by."

My earliest clients, older men and women, tended to view Social Security benefits almost as manna from heaven. Their gratitude often caused them to overestimate the financial power of their monthly government checks. In working with clients to plan for their future, I teach them to think of Social Security as one among other sources of income.

Social Security has lowered poverty rates. Americans sixty-five and older of every race rely on the program, and it has helped millions of black elders become more economically secure. Forty percent of African Americans sixty-five and older rely on Social Security as their sole source of income, and it provides income for 82.3 percent for all African Americans in that age group.

Elderly black women in particular have benefited. As a group they were highly affected by income inequity and child-care responsibilities that required them to leave the labor force for long periods and/or accept jobs with flexible schedules that offered no pensions. Rates of poverty among older black women would have more than doubled, rising to 66 percent, if it were not for Social Security, according to the Center on Budget and Policy Priorities.

African American elders passed on their confidence in the system to newer generations. Maybe you recall an elderly relative speaking positively about Social Security or President Roosevelt. After working with me, many of these older clients urged their children and grandchildren to begin planning for retirement. These younger generations expressed concern about rising costs and worries about how they would get by in future, but seldom did they view Social Security with alarm.

What a difference a few decades has made. Today few of my clients feel confident about the system. A national debate was ignited in 2004 when former Federal Reserve chairman Alan Greenspan warned that the government was promising more in retirement benefits than it was capable of providing in the future. He also warned that the Social Security system would be strained when the massive baby boomer population began retiring.

President George W. Bush soon proposed partial privatizing of Social Security, giving each worker a personalized investment account, with an opportunity to benefit from the high rates of return in the stock market. His idea sparked a public outcry. Keeping Social Security solvent will continue to be a subject of debate and worry.

An analysis by the Joint Center for Political and Economic Studies confirms the sea change in African American views on Social Security. From 1998 to 2005, the proportion of African Americans expecting Social Security to be their major source of retirement income fell from 35 to 29 percent. Among those earning more than $15,000 and less than $35,000, the proportion planning to rely on Social Security as a major source of income declined from 42 to 25 percent, and among African Americans earning more than $75,000, a mere 5 percent viewed it as a future major income source. When I lead financial-education sessions, no other subject generates more anxiety than Social Security. With that in mind, I have included the most frequently asked questions and my responses.

1. How does Social Security work?

The one thing most of us know about Social Security is that we've been paying for it since we got our first jobs. The next time you get a check, look at the list of deductions on your pay stub, and you'll see the abbreviation "FICA," which stands for Federal Insurance Contribution Act. FICA is a payroll tax. You pay a percentage of your income, and—if you work for someone else—your employer pays an equal amount. Since 2005, that percentage has been 6.2 percent for the worker, with the employer kicking in another 6.2 percent. If you're self-employed, then you pay the entire 12.4 percent.

> **PAYROLL TAX:**
> Named for FICA, the Federal Insurance Contribution Act, a tax deducted from salaries to finance Social Security

The money that's collected isn't put aside and saved for your future. It's spent on current Social Security recipients. That includes your mother, father, grandparents—anyone you know who's receiving monthly benefits now. Not all the money goes in one door and out the other. Some of the surplus is invested, and the federal government borrows the money to help pay for other programs—guaranteeing the loan with IOUs in the form of interest-paying Treasury bonds.

2. How do I qualify for Social Security?

Remember in school, how you could earn credits for taking a class? It's like that with Social Security. You're given one credit for every three months that you work. To get a credit, you have to earn at least $1,050 (this was the rate in 2008) during a three-month period such as January through March, or April through June. You can earn a maximum of four credits a year. When you have ten years of credits, a total of forty in all, you become vested. It's almost as if you're made a member of the Social Security club.

It may sound more complicated than it is. The Social Security Administration keeps track of your earnings through your Social Security number. Your benefits are based on an average of your lifetime earnings, along with a few adjustments. Everyone forty and older should expect to receive annual mailed statements of projected benefits. You can also request a copy online at www.social security.gov or by phoning the Social Security Administration at (800) 772–1213.

3. When will the Social Security Administration run out of money?

The image of the Social Security fund going bust made attention-grabbing headlines, but let's examine the truth behind the reports. It's true that our annual statements of projected Social Security benefits now include warnings from the Social Security commissioner that unless action is taken to strengthen the program, Social

Security will begin paying out more in benefits than are collected in taxes. It also states that without changes by the year 2040, the Social Security trust fund will be exhausted. A lot of people find this as frightening as the warning on cigarette packages. The problem with all the doom and gloom is that it blinds us to the facts.

There's good news and some not-so-good news. The best news of all is that people are living longer, and that's why the system is going to be strained. Maybe your grandparents or great-aunt, a favorite elder at your church, and hopefully you and all your loved ones, will live longer, thanks to medical breakthroughs. The U.S. Census Bureau reports that during the 1990s the number of people eighty-five and older increased by 38 percent. Is it any wonder that the Social Security system needs more money?

Another good-news reason the system needs increased funding is that since 1975, Social Security benefits have included a cost-of-living adjustment (COLA). Retirees receive automatic monetary increases to offset the effects of inflation on fixed incomes.

> **COSTS-OF-LIVING ADJUSTMENTS (COLAS):**
> Annual increases in income that help offset losses in purchasing power as prices rise

And the good news continues: If the money going into Social Security isn't increased immediately, we'll still be fine. There's enough to keep paying full Social Security benefits until 2040. Even then, it's not as if there won't be workers paying into the system; there will just be fewer of them because birthrates are lower. But we aren't talking about a handful of folks. The future labor force, comprising members of Generation X, the Echo Boom, and the iGeneration, is expected to keep enough FICA money flowing into the system to fund 70 to 75 percent of the scheduled benefit level until 2081. Keep in mind that I'm only talking about what would happen if the system isn't fixed, but I have every confidence that it will be. We can expect battles between the major political parties on the issue, but we will see reforms. Better sooner than later, of course.

Fixing the problem with Social Security is far from impossible. One idea being floated concerns changing the earnings cap, which in 2008 was $102,000. Anything earned over that amount was exempt from Social Security taxes. Eliminating the cap won't be popular with high-wage earners, but evidence suggests that this could close the shortfall. Other solutions—in addition to the contentious privatizing idea—include raising FICA taxes for employers and workers or increasing the retirement age again.

4. If the Social Security problem is fixable, why doesn't someone just fix it?

It's not only about politics, it's about policy, the solutions we come up with to fix problems. Politics and policy always intersect. And when it comes to Social Security, politicians don't want to offend the powerful senior-citizens lobby. They are a voting force to be reckoned with. So trying to "fix" Social Security is like playing hot potato. Remember that game? The potato burns your hands, and you pass it on as quickly as possible.

If you're wondering why some people want to completely restructure Social Security, consider the suggestion of raising the earnings cap. Like everyone else, folks in higher-income categories are trying to figure out how to hold on to their money. The wealthy have a lot of sway over politicians; not only do they vote, but they're also political donors. A lot of wealthy people think that they're being treated unfairly when it comes to Social Security. Overall, low-income individuals receive more in Social Security benefits than they pay in taxes. In 2007, the average retiree received 39 percent of preretirement income, while former high-income earners received an average of only 26 percent. Some conservatives believe that retirement saving is the responsibility of every individual and that they shouldn't have to help those who earn less.

Well-to-do individuals are more likely to understand investing, which is probably one of the primary ways they grew wealthy. To them, a system such as partial privatization might seem appealing because some of their FICA money would be deposited into an account that's earmarked for them to invest as they see fit.

Some Social Security change proponents are manipulating the situation, taking advantage of fear and the lack of financial education. After all, if you don't understand Social Security, you might not care how the system is fixed. And those who want to see change might reason that if they keep people fired up over the projected Social Security shortfall and distracted from the real issues, there's always a chance their way will win out.

5. Since African Americans have shorter life spans, shouldn't we retire early?

Statistically, those of us who make it to retirement age are expected to receive benefits for fewer years than white or Latino retirees, because we have a shorter life expectancy. But as African American leaders Hugh Price and Julian Bond pointed out in a *New York Times* opinion piece, one explanation for why black men have statistically shorter life spans than whites is because they are more likely to die when they are young. Once they reach sixty-five, the age gap narrows to only a two-year difference.

I work with statistics every day, but I don't let them rule my life. Think about it: If we made all our important decisions on the basis of what happens to some of the most vulnerable members of our race, then we couldn't step out of the house, because we might get shot. But then of course, we wouldn't have a house to step from, since fewer of us own homes. And accordingly, we could never hope to marry, and let's also forget about going to college or becoming a good parent, or leaving our kids a little something when we pass on. You get the point I'm trying to make.

If you're thinking about retiring early, it should be for a better reason than a number based on an arbitrary population group—and by the way, I don't even know what that means. But I do know about my health, and my lifestyle, and the genes I inherited from my parents and Grandma Chips, who is still kicking. I do take those factors into account when I'm thinking about my own mortality, but as with so much in life, there is always one answer: It depends on God.

However, when it comes to choosing when to start collecting Social Security benefits, it's up to you. This can be one of the most important decisions you'll ever make.

You can start claiming early benefits at the age of sixty-two, and receive about 70 percent of the full amount to which you're entitled. Depending on your birth year, you can get full benefits. If you were born between 1943 and 1954, you can start receiving full benefits at sixty-six. From that point the age limit increases by two months for each year (for instance, sixty-six and two months, sixty-six and four months). If you were born in 1960 or later, the full-benefit retirement age is sixty-seven.

The Social Security Administration uses the term "normal retirement age" to refer to the year you qualify for full retirement benefits. For specific information concerning your birth year and full retirement benefits, Google "Social Security" and your birth year, or call the toll-free Social Security number: (800) 772-1213.

Taking early and therefore lower benefits could mean that you receive less over the course of your lifetime. You can calculate your

break-even point by going online to www.socialsecurity.gov/
retire2/breakeven.htm.

> **NORMAL RETIREMENT AGE:**
> The age at which you can start receiving full retirement
> benefits as opposed to partial amounts

> **EARLY ELIGIBILITY:**
> Sixty-two is the age at which a qualified worker
> can begin collecting partial (permanent) benefits,
> regardless of normal retirement age

As a group, we are more likely than others to retire at sixty-two.
If you're considering applying for partial rather than full Social Security benefits, you should be aware that over the years, that 30
percent could make a big difference.

Joyce Lee, a fifty-nine-year-old nurse, can retire in three years
on partial benefits of about $959 a month. If she waits seven years,
until her normal retirement age, when she's sixty-six, her monthly
benefits come to about $1,272 a month. That's an extra $3,756 (not
including cost-of-living adjustments) a year for the rest of her life.
She chose the latter date, which makes sense for her. She's in good
health and is striking out on her own as a self-employed visiting
nurse. And should her plans change sometime soon, she can still
apply for the partial benefit. But she knew that if she had chosen
the early, reduced benefit, she would not be able to change her
mind. She would receive the reduced amount for the rest of her
life.

Here are examples of when it might be best to wait and claim full benefits:

- **You're healthy, you make an effort to stay that way, and your parents lived a long time—all of which increase the odds that you will, too.**

- **You can live comfortably on your savings or other income until you reach your full-retirement years.**

- **You plan to keep working and your income exceeds the Social Security earnings limit (the limit was $13,560 in 2008; you'll want to check this figure, since the amount is increased every year).** Keep in mind that "earnings" refers to income from work but not unearned money from pensions. Going over the limit, or failing the earnings test, as it's called, prior to normal retirement age, means you will be charged $1 for every $2 you earn over the earnings limit. You could wind up losing all your benefits for the year. If you wait until normal retirement age, there is no earnings test.

- **You're married and want to provide the most possible for the surviving spouse.** If the primary wage earner dies first, the survivor is entitled to 100 percent of the benefits that the deceased was receiving. At the same time, the lower-earning spouse can take his or her own benefits early without affecting future, perhaps higher, survivor benefits.

There are times when taking the early, reduced benefit can pay off. Here are some examples:

- You're ill and there's a good likelihood that you won't live much longer.

- You're planning to stop working, or already have, so you aren't worried about an earnings cap.

- You don't want to dip into your tax-deferred retirement savings.

- You have enough to live on comfortably but would like to save the benefits to pass along to your family as an inheritance, or you can use some of the benefits to buy a life-insurance benefit—which will be paid to your beneficiaries, income-tax free, upon your death.

6. Will I have to pay taxes on my Social Security benefits?

Yes. If you collect other income, you could wind up owing taxes on a portion of your Social Security benefits. The basic measurement is that you will pay taxes if the earnings income filed on your tax return is more than $25,000, or if you file a joint return and you and your spouse's total income is more than $32,000. Again, you will want to check for updated figures. For information on how much of your Social Security benefits will be taxed, consult a tax professional.

7. Are spouses entitled to a partner's Social Security benefits?

If you've been married at least a decade, you're entitled to collect benefits based on your own earnings record or half of what your spouse is entitled to, whichever is larger. If you decide to collect early spouse's benefits, your spouse is not required to also take early benefits, but the primary wage earner must start collecting benefits in order for the spouse to collect. Be aware that once you start taking early, reduced spousal benefits before your normal retirement age, your retirement benefit is reduced permanently. If you choose partial spouse's benefits, here's what you would get:

- **If your normal retirement age is sixty-five:** 37.5 percent of your spouse's benefit (without reducing your spouse's)

- **If your normal retirement age is sixty-six:** 35 percent of your spouse's benefit (without reducing your spouse's)

- **If your normal retirement age is sixty-seven:** 32.5 percent of your spouse's benefit (without reducing your spouse's)

If you begin collecting early, reduced benefits under your own work record, when your spouse retires later and starts collecting, you can switch and collect spousal benefits if they would be higher than your own. However, you will still receive reduced benefits because you began collecting early.

8. Can I get spousal benefits if I am divorced?
Yes. If you remained married for a decade or more, you can collect on an ex's Social Security record (without reducing his or her benefits) if the former spouse is receiving benefits or is deceased. There are further stipulations: You have to be unmarried, at least sixty-two years old, and not entitled to a higher benefit under your own work record.

If under your own record you are slated to receive less than your spousal benefits, when you begin collecting benefits, you will receive the higher spouse's amount.

If you apply for early, reduced benefits, the Social Security Administration will check to see if you are eligible for your own retirement benefits and for spousal benefits. You'll receive your own first, and if scheduled for more government income, you'll receive a combination of benefits equaling the higher, spouse's benefit. You cannot receive this benefit until your ex-spouse files for retirement.

Social Security also provides income for the families of workers who die. Collecting early retirement benefits does not reduce your survivor benefits as long as you are at least of normal retirement age when you begin collecting them.

For more information on filing for spouse's benefits, go online to www.socialsecurity.gov/applyforbenefits. To locate a Social Security office, go online to www.socialsecurity.gov/locator or phone (800) 772-1213 for more information.

HELPFUL HINT

If you have not already done so, look closely at your Social Security statement, particularly the "Your Estimated Benefits" section on page 2. Please pay attention also to your disability information to learn whether you have earned sufficient credits to qualify for this benefit.

BUILDING FINANCIAL LITERACY

To the uninitiated, a portfolio is simply a portable case for holding loose papers. But when investment-savvy people refer to a *portfolio*, they are talking about the investments they hold, such as stocks, bonds, and mutual funds.

As you continue working through this book, you may want to consider building a portfolio of your own or adding to a preexisting one.

CONSIDERING SCRIPTURE

"Because you know that the testing of your faith produces endurance; and let endurance have its full effect, so that you may be mature and complete, lacking in nothing."   —James 1:3–4.

If the spirit moves you, read this passage aloud and write about its meaning as you become more financially literate.

_____

_____

_____

_____

_____

_____

11

Choosing Traditional or Roth IRAs

At twenty-three, Kimberly Addison, an advertising manager at a radio station, represents a growing segment of my practice—people thirty and younger. It used to be that folks her age didn't want to contemplate reaching forty, much less retirement. But something exciting is happening that is connected to what lots of young people *do* and *don't* have.

After two years of working, Ms. Addison earns more than her mom did at twice her age. But what her mom has and Ms. Addison doesn't is a traditional pension that guarantees income for life. Ms. Addison says, "I had lots of job offers. My mom told me to hold out until a company sweetened the pot with a pension. That didn't happen. . . . I love my job, but I'm seriously jealous when I see the monthly checks my mom gets for the rest of her life, now that she's retired. I call what I feel 'pension envy.'"

A lot of workers know where she's coming from. Many employers offer retirement benefits that are "qualified" or "nonquali-

> ## QUALIFIED RETIREMENT PLAN:
> With this 401(k)-type plan, money is deducted on a pretax or after-tax basis directly from an employee's salary

> ## NONQUALIFIED RETIREMENT PLAN:
> Under these plans, executives and other top-earning employees may be given after-tax rewards in the form of cash, stock, stock options, and so on

fied." To be qualified a plan has to meet certain federal guidelines. Whether it's the employee or the employer funding the account, the earnings gained are tax-deferred until they're paid out. Nonqualified means that the government does not limit or restrict the benefit. Ms. Addison and her mom both have qualified retirement plans, but these plans are very different from each other.

Ms. Addison's mom has what is known in the financial field as a defined benefit (DB), which is a fully funded pension plan. Before retiring she received a statement that defined the specific sums and benefits she could expect, based on her length of service and final salary, if she continued working for the company. Her employer assumed all the financial risks. The benefits were paid for from the profits her company's fund manager made investing on her behalf and that of other employees.

A growing number of companies are dropping or freezing DB pension plans. Two thirds of employers that offer DB pensions have closed their plans to new employees, frozen them for all workers, or plan to do so in the near future. IBM, Lockheed Martin, General Motors, Sprint Nextel, and Verizon have frozen their DB plans.

> **DEFINED BENEFIT PLAN:**
> An employer-provided traditional pension in which the employee receives a specific monthly payment

> **DEFINED-CONTRIBUTION PLAN:**
> Employees contribute to a job-related retirement vehicle

They will keep paying benefits to their retirees, and existing employees will continue to accrue benefits, but the plan is closed to new employees.

The decline in the prevalence of DB pension plans is quite dramatic. In 1987, among Americans with retirement plans, 62 percent had traditional or defined benefits. By 2007, that number had dwindled to 19 percent, according to a Boston College study. This decline in benefits will affect African Americans disproportionately, since more of us tend to work in government jobs, which are more likely to offer pensions. The proportion of African American men receiving pensions is slightly higher than that of all older people, while African American women receive a lower number of defined benefits proportionately. In an Ariel/Schwab survey of high-income blacks, two thirds of black participants, compared with about half of the employed white participants, had employers that offered traditional pension plans.

The downsizing of corporate retirement benefits signals changing attitudes about who should be responsible for funding and managing employee accounts. Many employers now offer defined-contribution (DC) plans that make no promises of an income. Employees can defer a percentage of their salary for a 401(k)-style savings plan, and the company might match a small percentage of the contributions. With DC plans, there are no guaranteed monthly payouts at retirement, the employee bears the investment risk, and the size of the nest egg depends on the amount the employee has contributed. From 1980 to 1999, the percentage of eligible workers participating in DC plans skyrocketed, from 17 to 58 percent.

The demise of pensions and the workforce shift from defined benefits to defined contributions helps explain why I'm working with more young clients. When I opened my doors in 1993, many major employers were still providing lifetime benefits, and often employees didn't familiarize themselves with their pensions until they were facing retirement.

Today, with an eye to encouraging workers to save for their future and hoping to reduce reliance on government programs, legislators have pushed through a law designed to stabilize the pension system—the 2006 Pension Protection Act, which took effect in 2008. This law encourages employers to automatically enroll workers in retirement investment plans, set levels for contribution amounts, and provide investment advice.

That's where I come into the retirement picture for an increasing number of workers. The City of Richmond and various departments for the State of Virginia have asked me to lead financial-education sessions for their employees.

These audiences often include an array of ages, and I find among younger workers that taking the hands-on approach to managing their accounts is sparking an early interest in financial literacy. One of the most important terms for workers to learn is *individual retirement accounts* (IRAs). I often explain these by saying that if you were driving down a road and heard on the radio that a big storm was approaching, you would probably seek shelter. The approaching storm I'm referring to is the future, with its unknown aspects:

how long we might live and the fact that we can no longer count on traditional sources for lifetime income. That's why we need a financial shelter, which brings us to IRAs. Simply put, they are tax shelters that allow people to save for the future.

IRAs are qualified plans. They're personal tax shelters, as opposed to employer-sponsored plans, and beneath these shelters there might be stocks, bonds, real estate, and other investments. The two types of IRAs are traditional and Roth, the latter named for its chief legislative sponsor, former U.S. senator William V. Roth, Jr., of Delaware.

> **TRADITIONAL IRA:**
> A retirement account in which contributions are tax-deductible at the time they are made and earnings grow tax-free until withdrawal. These entail a required minimum distribution after age seventy and a half.

> **ROTH IRA:**
> A retirement account in which contributions are not tax-deductible but can be collected tax-free at the age of fifty-nine and a half

I can illustrate the difference between the IRAs by returning to Kimberly Addison, who initially contributed $50 a month to her retirement account. She chose to shelter her money in a Roth IRA. Why? Technically the Roth is a tax-free account, but you don't reap the rewards of the tax-free benefit until you're fifty-nine and a half and have owned it for at least five years.

A Roth can be good news for people of all ages. Young people beginning their careers are usually earning less than they will be making in the future. Ms. Addison will forgo a tax savings now, but forty years hence, when she withdraws money from her IRA, she will likely be in a higher income-tax bracket because she'll be earning substantially more. If she has a Roth, she will not be taxed on the money when she begins withdrawing it.

The flexible withdrawal rules of a Roth IRA are another reason that they're considered an attractive investment for young people. After her account has been opened for a minimum of five years, Ms. Addison can withdraw up to $10,000 for the purchase of a first home without having to pay tax penalties. (This benefit does not apply to a 401(k)-type of plan.) On Roth IRAs there are also exceptions made on withdrawals for medical expenses and higher education. But I recommend leaving contributions in an IRA until retirement. The longer you can leave the money in your account, the more you'll have when you withdraw it.

Before I met Ms. Addison's mother, Katherine—often referred to as "Ms. Kat," by those who know her—she had opened a traditional IRA. The word *tradition* comes from the Latin *traditio*, which refers to handing down, as in passing along from one generation to the next. In fact, Ms. Kat was determined to start a new tradition in her family, teaching her daughter financial literacy, so she could one day pass that knowledge on to her own children.

Ms. Kat chose the traditional IRA. Her income was high and she needed a tax break so she could hold on to as much cash as possible. She was raising her daughter on her own. With traditional IRAs, taxes are deferred until the money is withdrawn. For those seeking to save on taxes, the traditional IRA has a long window of purchase time. To qualify for a 2008 income tax reduction, for instance, an individual could purchase a traditional IRA from January 1, 2008, up through April 15, 2009.

In 2008 both the traditional and the Roth had contribution limits of $5,000 a year for individuals and, for married couples, $5,000 per spouse, for a total of $10,000 per household. A catch-up provision for those fifty and older increased the contribution limit to $6,000 per individual and $12,000 per couple.

The greatest benefit of investing in a traditional IRA is that your contributions are tax-deductible. I only recommend the traditional IRA to clients who are excellent at keeping up with deadlines because it has a tricky feature that requires account holders to start withdrawing an IRS-specified amount by April 1 of the year after the owners turn seventy and a half, even if still employed. This provision is known as the required minimum distribution (RMD). If you ignore the RMD date, the IRS will charge you an excess-accumulation tax of 50 percent on the amount you should have withdrawn. For instance, if you were supposed to have withdrawn $30,000 and did not, your penalty will be $15,000. I've worked with many clients who came to me after incurring this penalty. But that's only one reason that I almost always recommend the Roth IRA instead of the traditional.

> **REQUIRED MINIMUM DISTRIBUTION:**
> Annual minimum IRA withdrawal required by the IRS

Why I Love Roth IRAs

- **They are ideal for everyone.** The fact that employee contributions can be collected tax-free at the age of fifty-nine and a half is not the only reason I often recommend Roth IRAs. They are available to anyone, regardless of age, who has earned income. Please note, however, that at the time of this writing, there is a Roth income limit: If you earn $116,000 or more (gross income) per year, or $169,000 or more for married couples, you cannot contribute to a Roth IRA. But these figures increase from year to year, so check with your financial institution or financial adviser for the current contribution amounts and income-restriction levels. As of 2010, a law will go into effect that makes conversions to Roth IRAs available without income restrictions. Contributions will still have income limits.

- **There are no minimum-distribution requirements.** Not at seventy and a half or any age, and as long as you're still working, you can continue to contribute to your Roth.

- **Gains are not subject to income tax.** Although your contributions are not tax-deductible, earnings are tax-deferred and qualified withdrawals are free of federal income tax if you're over age fifty-nine and a half. This is the most important feature of all. There is a widespread misconception that most retirees are in a lower tax bracket. That's not necessarily the case—and it is more than likely that tax rates will go up. Let's say a couple's retirement savings has grown to $1.5 million in a traditional IRA and they want to withdraw $50,000 a year for thirty years. They would wind up paying Uncle Sam $18,000 with each withdrawal (and have $32,000 to spend). Over three decades, they'd wind up paying $540,000 in taxes! On the other hand, if they had instead purchased a Roth, forgoing the immediate tax deduction, they could be withdrawing that $50,000 a year tax-free.

THE BEAUTY OF 401(K) ROTHS

If your company is offering a 401(k)-type Roth, sign up. Withdrawals on ordinary 401(k)-type plans are subject to income tax, but that's not the case with these new Roth 401(k) plans, which became available in 2006. You won't get up-front tax savings that you get from contributions to a regular 401(k) plan, but down the road, when your money has grown and if you're in a higher tax bracket, this tax savings will be greater than deductions you receive today. The 2008 contribution limits for these accounts are $15,500 and $20,500 for those fifty and older. If your company is not offering the Roth 401(k)-type option, try to convince your human resources specialist to get the ball rolling.

401(k)-type funds can be converted to IRAs. There are no income limits on Roth 401(k)s. You can use a direct rollover to convert your employer-sponsored plan, such as the 401(k), to the traditional or Roth IRA. Ken Samuels, a fifty-seven-year-old medical technician, had a half-million-dollar 401(k) account. He wanted to retire and start living off his money in two years. Three years earlier, on my advice, he had set up a Roth, so he was able to roll his money into that account. Now he only has to wait two years for the Roth five-year-before-withdrawal period. He will have to pay taxes up front, but by rolling his retirement money into a Roth, Mr. Samuels can later withdraw tax-free money. People earning more than $100,000 do not qualify for a Roth conversion. Again, that income requirement will be alleviated in 2010.

If you're a candidate for a Roth conversion, talk to a financial adviser about the best way to pay off the penalty.

Although there's a five-year waiting period before you can withdraw money from a Roth, the clock starts ticking the minute you open your account. So my advice is to get a Roth IRA now. You can get them at many financial institutions.

HELPFUL HINT

Use online stores to lower your costs on products you buy in large quantities. Discount online businesses include www.overstock.com and www.SmartBargains .com. Also, before purchasing big-ticket items, research them on the Consumer Reports website at www.con sumerreportsonline.com, so you can get the highest quality for your money. You can sign up for Consumer Reports for short or longer periods.

BUILDING FINANCIAL LITERACY

Americans who remember President Gerald Ford as the accident-prone chief executive might not realize that in 1974 he signed into law the Employee Retirement Income Security Act (ERISA), which marked a turning point in the funding of pension plans. Through ERISA Congress was able to take a hands-on approach to private pensions.

PENSION BENEFIT GUARANTY CORPORATION:
The federal agency that keeps benefits flowing to retirees if employers default

ERISA:
Federal laws that oversee private-industry retirement plans

ERISA has been amended many times, in the process providing for many of the after-tax incentives that encourage retirement investments. Under ERISA the federal government also established the Pension Benefit Guaranty Corporation to insure private pensions. Were it not for the Pension Benefit Guaranty Corporation, thousands of steel, airline, and auto-parts employees might have been stranded during their senior years after their employers declared bankruptcy. Thanks to the PBGC, pensioners continued to receive benefits—although some of those benefits were lower than they would have been had the companies continued operating. ERISA and Internal Revenue Section 401(a) provided for qualified and nonqualified plans.

CONSIDERING SCRIPTURE

"Now to Him who by the power at work within us is able to accomplish abundantly far more than all we can ask or imagine." **—Ephesians 3:20.**
If the spirit moves you, read this passage aloud and write about its meaning as you become more financially literate.

_____

_____

_____

_____

_____

12

Recognizing an Annuity for What It Is

Perhaps you've seen the television ad that I'm about to describe.

A businessman's retirement party is ending, and as he steps onto an elevator, an eight-hundred-pound gorilla suggests that he consider buying an annuity.

If you have seen this commercial, there's a chance that you didn't understand what the heck that gorilla was talking about. You might still be wondering, What the heck *is* an annuity?

The fact is, annuities are all around us. Lots of people you know couldn't survive comfortably after retiring without them. The best-known annuities are Social Security checks. And then there are the traditional pensions that we discussed in the previous chapter.

The word *annuity* derives from the Latin root for *annual* and generally refers to any recurring, periodic series of payments. The gorilla in the commercial isn't talking about a company pension or Social Security. It is referring to a commercial annuity, which an individual purchases from an insurance company in exchange for income that can be paid out immediately or at a future date. Annuity policyholders receive payments from a combination of the untaxed principal, which is the money originally invested, and the capital, the money or property used to generate more wealth.

If you're planning for the future, a commercial annuity might be one of the most important tools you can use to create peace of mind. This pay-for-it-yourself benefit can supplement Social Security or a company pension. Many of my retired clients rely on all three—Social Security, a company pension, and a commerical annuity—for income. Others purchase commercial annuities as stand-alone pensions in the absence of any other lifetime income.

I don't recommend annuities to the following clients:

1. Lower-income clients who can afford to live on their Social Security or pension plans

2. Those who would have to spend more than half of their savings to purchase the policy

3. People who are already retired

Commercial annuities can benefit many people: the struggling divorcée who never worked outside the home because she was raising children; the relatively low-income worker who realizes that Social Security will not be enough to live on; the entrepreneur who has never drawn a regular salary and has no Social Security; and the wealthy client who wants to fill in the financial gap between what she has coming in and what she needs.

The popularity of commercial annuities seems destined to increase. As more companies pull traditional pensions off the table and millions of baby boomers head into retirement, folks are going to discover that there's something highly valuable out there that they've been overlooking. There are signs that this is already occurring. In 2006 a MetLife Mature Market Institute study found that a third of current retirees already relied on commercial annuities. Please consider them among your options as you progress toward your retirement goals. This chapter can help you understand what an annuity is so you can make an informed decision about whether to purchase one.

Unlike life insurance, which doesn't pay off until the policyholder dies, with annuities, the longer the policyholder lives, the more money he receives over time. Here's how it works: You either make a series of payments or hand over a lump sum, in exchange for which the company agrees to send you paychecks for the rest of your life or an agreed-upon number of years. The company invests the money, and after a specified period the accumulated funds are paid out. Money from commercial annuities can make the difference in the quality of a retiree's life. That MetLife study I mentioned earlier found that retirees who receive commercial annuity payments in addition to Social Security and pension are three times more likely to describe retirement as better than they expected it would be.

The amount you pay into the annuity determines how much you'll get monthly. For example, if you're a sixty-five-year-old male and have invested $100,000 into what is referred to as a "fixed" immediate annuity, you would get about $655.58 a month from the insurer. If you're wondering whether this is a good deal, imagine that instead of purchasing an annuity, you deposited that money into a savings account and received monthly payments back. That $100,000 would run out in approximately twelve years, when you reached the age of seventy-seven.

If instead you put the money into an annuity, you would continue receiving checks as long as you live. So those same numbers begin to look quite different. If you lived, for example, until the age of eighty-five, and you receive $713 a month, or $8,556 a year, and if you're retired for twenty years, you will receive a total of $171,120. Depending upon the type of annuity you selected, if you die before the amount of your contribution is paid out, your heirs may inherit the balance.

There are many kinds of commercial annuities. As consumer demand increases, companies are introducing improved products with flexible payment options and payouts. Even in this favorable market, however, buying an annuity is best done with professional advice. To deepen your understanding of commercial annuities, let's look at two of my clients.

Client Profile

HADDIE SIMMONS: sixty-nine, a single, retired teacher, no children.

WHAT WAS AT ISSUE: Ms. Simmons's retirement plans were thrown into disarray, and she needed a higher monthly income than she had orginally assumed.

DETAILS OF HER STORY: This Mississippi native had settled into a comfortable retirement. She was volunteering at her church's literacy project and enjoying vacations in Hawaii, Brazil, and Nigeria. Then her home was destroyed by Hurricane Katrina. Vowing to never again live near a coastline, she returned to Richmond, where she'd lived and worked for much of her adult life.

A friend suggested that Ms. Simmons come to see me, and at our first meeting Ms. Simmons said, "I can't complain. I survived, praise God. A lot of people didn't. But I'm scared that I won't have enough money to last the rest of my life." With her house in a shambles, she was unable to put it on the market. Meanwhile, her bills were mounting. Although the mortgage on her Mississippi house was paid, she was renting an apartment in Virginia, and she wanted to buy a condominium.

WHAT SHE DECIDED ON: An immediate fixed annuity.

UNDERSTANDING IMMEDIATE FIXED ANNUITIES: An immediate annuity is an insurance policy in which in exchange for a lump sum, the company makes a series of payments, which begin soon after the contract is signed. *Fixed* means "unchanging"; the insurer determines up front how much money the policyholder will receive each month.

Why an immediate fixed annuity worked for her:

- **She could afford to pay an up-front lump sum.** Since payouts began immediately, Ms. Simmons had to give the insurer a lump sum. In a direct rollover, she transferred $150,000—half of her tax-deferred savings—into the immediate fixed annuity. In return she began to receive $1,045 a month, approximately 28 percent of which was taxable. These payments will continue for her lifetime.

- **She was over sixty-five.** Immediate annuities are better suited for individuals who are well into their retirement, ages sixty-five to eighty-five, and who need more income.

- **She wanted stable payments.** She wanted to know to the penny how much she would receive each month. After her experience with Hurricane Katrina, she had an aversion to taking risks. The rule in investing is that the lower the risk, the lower your return. Immediate fixed annuities, which are relatively safe, don't yield high returns. The money contributed by the policyholder is invested in bonds, bond funds, and the insurer's general accounts, all of which pay low interest rates, generally about 3 to 6 percent. This is not an investment for someone highly concerned with inflation rates.

Those who are concerned about keeping up with inflation and who seek opportunities for greater returns might want to consider *variable immediate annuities*. These also require lump-sum investments (since the payouts begin immediately), but rather than the policyholder receiving fixed amounts, the amounts paid are subject to change. The monthly payments vary because they are tied to stock-market-based subaccounts. As the stock market goes, so goes the monthly payment. If the market fares well, the policyholder receives an increase in income. If the market goes down, the check is for a lesser amount. This doesn't mean the company can lower payments dramatically. You should buy policies only from companies that offer a clause stipulating that your check won't go below a certain amount.

- **She wanted her monthly payments to be as high as possible and had no interest in leaving behind wealth for anyone else.** She chose a policy called an *immediate single-life fixed annuity*, in which only the policyholder's life is covered, and the money will not be passed on to heirs. If she had wanted to pass any balance of her account, she would have received a lower monthly rate. But, God forbid, if Ms. Simmons died at seventy-five, after receiving $1,045 a month or $12,540 annually for six years, that would total $75,240. The insurer would keep the $74,760 balance as gains realized on her original investment. Fortunately, Ms. Simmons is in good health, and her mother is still alive at ninety. If she follows in her mother's footsteps and lives to be ninety, she will continue to receive $12,540 annually for twenty-one years, which comes to $263,340.

A lot of people steer clear of immediate fixed annuities because they want to leave their money to family members, not insurance companies, and that has opened the way for a new payout option, the "life-with-refund" option. This means that if you are willing to accept lower monthly checks, you can buy an immediate annuity with a stipulation that if you die before you have received the amount of your original investment, your heirs get the balance. Your beneficiaries will be taxed at their ordinary tax rates.

When you take out an immediate annuity (whether fixed or variable), the older you are, the higher your monthly payout, because the insurance company is betting that you will die soon. For that reason, an eighty-year-old will get a larger monthly check than a sixty-year-old. So the amount of the policyholder's "paycheck" on an immediate annuity is determined by the dollar amount contributed and on the basis of age. An insurance-company actuary—trained in statistics, accounting, and mathematics—determines policy rates—by looking at life-expectancy patterns in the United States. Women tend to live longer than men. At the time of this writing, life expectancy is 69.8 years for black males and 76.5 years for black females.

Under the same logic, monthly payouts on immediate fixed annuities are higher for people who have a lot of medical issues. This is the reverse of the way a life insurance policy works, when a company might decline to accept an individual because they think he or she won't live for many years. In these situations, as always, I'm delighted when clients live decades beyond what was calculated.

Client Profile

JAMES AND ERNESTINE WILLIAMS: He is forty-four and works as a musician. She is forty-one and is employed as a radiology technician. They have two children, ages fourteen and twelve.

WHAT WAS AT ISSUE: She contributes to a hospital-sponsored retirement savings plan and to Social Security. Mr. Williams is not vested in the Social Security system and has no retirement savings. They're worried about how they'll survive after she retires.

DETAILS OF THEIR STORY: With two children and one steady paycheck, the couple works together to, as they put it, "keep the wolf away from our door." But they are committed to getting into the black and staying there. They've paid off credit card debt with money Mr. Williams now earns from giving music lessons, and they have cut back on their spending. She has increased contributions to her company-sponsored retirement savings plan and has purchased a Roth IRA. But they've identified a gap of $6,000 annually between what they want to live on in retirement and what they'll have coming in.

WHAT THEY CHOSE TO CLOSE THE GAP: A deferred annuity. As *deferred* suggests, the payments that the couple receives won't begin until a future date. As with Social Security, the payments are delayed until the policyholder chooses to receive them.

> DEFERRED ANNUITY:
> An investment in which payments on tax-deferred earnings are delayed until the policyholder chooses to receive them

Why a deferred annuity worked for them:

- **They didn't have a lump sum to contribute.** Although this type of account can be opened with a lump sum, it doesn't have to be. The couple was starting early enough so that it was practical for them to make monthly payments toward their goal of accumulating $200,000 in an annuity. They are paying $250 a month, and they have twenty-four years to get there. They hope that in years to come, after they have raised their children, they will have more money available and can increase their payments.

- **They want to save on taxes.** This is one of the chief advantages for choosing a deferred annuity—it's a tax shelter. Whatever the Williamses earn with their annuity is tax-deferred. With a fixed or variable deferred annuity, you don't have to pay taxes until you use it.

- **They want to keep pace with inflation.** The Williamses chose a *variable* deferred annuity in which payments fluctuate based on the performance of the stock market.

> VARIABLE DEFERRED ANNUITY:
>
> A tax-sheltered investment sponsored by an insurance company in which income fluctuates based on the performance of the stock market

This couple has many years before they retire. They realize that the stock market will fluctuate but that in the long run their variable deferred annuity will give them an opportunity for greater growth. Those averse to risk and who are more comfortable with lower payouts can choose fixed deferred annuities.

- **They worry about running out of money.** By the time their account has grown to $200,000, they will still be willing to take some risk on market fluctuations. This can work to their advantage.* Here's how I imagine their situation unfolding:

1. After retirement, they receive monthly payments on the annuity. They have chosen a company that offers them monthly payments based on 6 percent of their balance, which is $12,000 a year or $1,000 a month. Companies offer various payout percentages, Offers vary based on prevailing interest rates and the individual's age and gender. I'm going to digress from the Williamses with the following example.

   I worked with an eighty-four-year-old retired surgeon who wanted to invest $500,000 in a deferred variable annuity. She wanted the highest payout possible to supplement her other sources of income. When I requested annuity offers, some company bids came in at 6 and 7 percent for her monthly payout. In the end, a solid firm offered 9 percent. She will be paid no less than $45,000 a year and possibly more for the rest of her life. The older you are, the higher the percentage offered, because the companies assume you aren't going to live that much longer. Had this physician been sixty-five

---

* Positive results are not guaranteed when investing in equities. Investing involves risk, including loss of principal.

rather than eighty-four, the payout bids would have been lower. This physician's contract also stipulated that the balance of her contribution would be passed on to her heirs. The message here is to shop around for the best offers. Now back to the Williamses.

2. One year into Mr. and Mrs. Williams's retirement, they will have received $1,000 monthly annuity payouts, which means they'll have withdrawn $12,000. But now the stock market has gone up, and the value of their account has increased; it is now worth $250,000.* If they're still drawing down 6 percent, that means they'll now get monthly checks of $1,250.

3. Let's assume that things go well in the stock market every year for the first four years, and by the fifth year after retirement, their account is worth $350,000. By now, 6 percent of their account is $1,750 a month. They started off receiving $1,000 a month, but they are now getting $1,750 and keeping pace with inflation.

4. But let's imagine that in the fifth year the financial markets go sour; the major corporations are doing poorly, and the account drops from $350,000 to $260,000. With a variable deferred annuity, the policyholders don't have to take the loss because their income is protected. The Williamses will get

---

* Past performance is no guarantee of future results. The stock market involves risks, including loss of principal.

that high-water mark of $1,750 for the rest of their lives. The amount is locked in.

5. If the account goes up again, the Williamses' monthly income goes up with it. If they're in their eighth decade and the account has grown to $440,000, at 6 percent withdrawal they will be receiving $2,200 a month.

- **They want their children to inherit wealth.** The balance of their original contribution will be paid to their beneficiaries.

IF YOU DECIDE TO BUY AN ANNUITY, PROCEED WITH CAUTION

Many of my clients feel that the peace of mind provided by commercial annuities is worth any price, but that doesn't mean they shouldn't be aggressive about finding policies that fit their needs. Be sure not to sign anything until you have worked with a professional who helps explain the fine print. A few other caveats follow:

Consider your time line

Commercial annuities can be a blessing or a curse, depending on whether you find a policy that's right for you and whether it makes sense for someone in your income bracket. Over one third of all cases involving financial exploitation of the elderly involve annuity sales, according to the North American Securities Administration Association. Once you've found a trusted adviser, ask how an annuity might fit your needs. For instance, if you're sixty-five or older, an immediate annuity might make the most sense. With deferred annuities, you might not be able to use the money in your account for several years. Can you afford to wait? That's the kind of question you'll want answered before you sign on the dotted line.

Ask about surrender charges

Be sure to inquire about "liquidity features" before you purchase any annuity. That means you want to know whether you will be charged for pulling your money out of an annuity shortly after you invest it. Some but not all commercial annuities include a surrender charge. If you choose a policy with a surrender fee, here's how it would affect you. Let's say you invest $100,000 in an annuity that has a four-year, 4 percent surrender charge. Within that four-year period you will be allowed to withdraw 10 percent of the value per year without incurring a charge. If you withdraw an additional $10,000 within that same year, you will pay a 4 percent surrender charge of $400. In the second year, the surrender charge is reduced to 3 percent, and it continues to go down each year until the fourth year, after which the charges cease. In working with a financial professional, you will want to get clear answers in writing concerning any surrender charges and payout terms.

Be aware that, as with other retirement plans, if you withdraw money from an annuity before you are fifty-nine and a half you will be charged a 10 percent IRS penalty. You'll notice that this chapter is replete with warnings, but that doesn't lessen my belief that for some people, the right annuities can be a blessing.

HELPFUL HINT

Because annuity insurers guarantee payments, you will want to research the financial health of a company before you sign a contract. Even if you don't purchase an annuity, you should know how to research insurance companies and their histories of meeting financial obli-

gations. **You can learn by researching a company you are already using for insurance coverage.**

1. Go to the free online website www.standardandpoors .com.

2. Register. (Under "Company Name," you can enter "self." If you don't want to be contacted, click the check-marks to remove your name from the company's e-mail, phone, and mail lists.)

3. Go to "My Homepage."

4. Go to "Products and Services," and from the drop-down box choose "Ratings."

5. To the left of the screen, click on "Credit Ratings Search."

6. At "Search by Organization Name," under "Keyword," enter your company's name. The highest rating is AAA (triple A) and the lowest is BBB- (triple B-minus).

Although a trusted financial professional can be an excellent source of advice, rely on your own instincts and do your homework before you make any financial decisions.

BUILDING FINANCIAL LITERACY

NASDAQ may sound like the stock-car racing association (that's NASCAR), but you don't want to get them confused or you'll wind up far from the beaten track after you start investing. NASDAQ stands for the National Association of Securities Dealers Automated Quotation System. Listen to the nightly business news and you'll get used to hearing the word, which refers to an electronic means of providing price quotations to stock market participants.

CONSIDERING SCRIPTURE

"Send out your bread upon the waters, for after many days you will get it back." **—Ecclesiastes 11:1.** **If the spirit moves you, read this passage aloud and write about its meaning as you become more financially literate.**

_____

_____

_____

_____

_____

_____

_____

STEP 6

View Home Ownership
as a Viable Option

13

Understanding Our Passion for Real Estate

Cheryl Brooks, a thirty-three-year-old attorney, represents another segment of my clientele—black professional women, whose numbers are growing ever more impressive in the United States. A 2005 article in the *Journal of Blacks in Higher Education*, on increases in the numbers of black students graduating from college, points out that over a period of fifteen years, graduation rates for black women made steady gains, with college completion rates rising from 34 percent in 1990 to 46 percent by 2005.

Once they become financially secure, many of my clients, like a number of other single, professional women, want to purchase homes because they want to have property of their own, something to rely on when they're retired. When Ms. Brooks began working with me, shortly after making partner in her law firm, she explained that she had been very excited about buying a house. She added, "I was a foster child and never felt at home anywhere. Having a place of my own would be very meaningful."

Her enthusiasm was dampened by the mortgage crisis that be-gan unfolding in 2006, when a rising tide of U.S. home owners, unable to continue making mortgage payments, hit rock bottom and their properties were seized in foreclosures. A disproportion-ate number of the people who lost their homes were black.

"I drove through a fairly new neighborhood in Cleveland," Ms. Brooks said. "I couldn't believe how many houses had been aban-doned. Someone told me that home owners were so frightened by their ballooning mortgages, they grabbed what they could and ran." She stared past me, as if distracted by a memory. "In Cleveland, I lived in a foster home with a woman who took me in along with others, but not for humanitarian reasons. She told us kids that she needed the stipend to pay her mortgage. Her house meant every-thing to her, as if it could protect her from becoming destitute in old age."

Ms. Brooks spoke through clenched teeth. "I drove down her street the other day and saw the house—I won't call it a home—where I spent five miserable years. There were strangers out front and I stopped to ask about her. They said she took out a second mortgage and lost everything." Ms. Brooks fanned herself with a glossy bro-chure from the sales office of a new housing subdivision. She looked furious as she recalled the details.

"Aaron, I sacrificed to get this far. I need your advice. I've heard that people do better when they invest in the stock market, and that a house appreciates at a much lower rate, especially once you start paying for repairs, real estate taxes, and home owner's insur-ance. I don't want to put my money into a house and find out later that I made a mistake. Is purchasing a home still a good idea for someone who's thinking about the future?"

I was glad she asked. As African Americans, we put a lot of trust in real estate. A 2006 Ariel Mutual Funds/Charles Schwab Black In-vestor Study comparing the financial attitudes of higher-income blacks and whites found that twice as many blacks as whites (34 percent versus 16 percent) said they were saving to buy real estate, start a business, or both. Additionally, more blacks than whites owned real estate apart from their own homes (42 percent versus 33 percent). They expect these investments to help fund their retirement.

Attitudes such as these have led many of us to invest in real estate. In 1994, less than 43 percent of African Americans owned homes. Ten years later, almost 50 percent of us did, according to Harvard University's Joint Center for Housing Studies. Young African Americans made many of those home purchases, but those of us fifty-five and older were still much more likely to own homes. Because so many of us rely on purchasing real estate, I have devoted two chapters to this very significant subject.

There's no telling how many of us will alter our retirement plans as a result of the national mortgage meltdown, which left more than a million households—people of various races—facing foreclosure. As devastating as it may be for those who lost their homes, I hope their experiences will generate a discussion in our community that increases our financial knowledge. It's important to gain insight into the larger issues that affect our ability to thrive.

You recall that in the past, when people applied for mortgages, they went to the closest savings and loan. If their applications were approved, they were in a sense borrowing from neighbors who deposited money at the same institutions, which had a stake in whether the loans were paid off. Many local institutions also sold their home loans to the Federal Home Loan Mortgage Corporation (Freddie Mac) and the Federal National Mortgage Association (Fannie Mae), government-sponsored entities that were created to make home ownership available to low-moderate and middle-income consumers.

In today's global economy, financial businesses operate in a markedly different fashion than in the past.* Around the globe, people, corporations, and nations are making more money than they can spend. We might hear that some hedge funds have billions of dollars or that China's success as an exporter has given that nation a trade surplus of $1 trillion. Although that might not seem to have anything to do with us, it does. Money can't be eaten or buried. If it's expected to grow, it must be invested. You'd be right on target if you pictured money flowing across borders, from financial institutions located in places like Caracas, Venezuela; Lagos, Nigeria; Riyadh, Saudi Arabia; and New York City. Some of those dollars found their way into cheap mortgages in cities such as Oakland, Detroit, and Chicago, obtained by ordinary people.

Perhaps you have seen news photos of people standing dejectedly in front of their repossessed homes. We might not know much about these folks, but it's safe to assume that they were chasing the American dream of home ownership and that they were often uneducated about the mortgage process. With little financial experience, they were no match for the brokers trolling their neighborhoods or the telemarketers who called to offer houses for no money down and low monthly payments. The competition grew so fierce among brokers that there are stories of borrowers qualifying for loans without proof of employment, income, or rental history.

Most of these loans were subprime, which means the borrowers were considered less than desirable loan candidates by their lending institutions. Subprime loans don't always lead to financial

* I am grateful to economist Gerald Harris, founder of Harris Planning and Strategy Consulting, of San Francisco, California, and Nancy Lehrkind, a Grubb Company Realtor/attorney in Piedmont, California, both of whom shared their expertise on real estate and the global market.

ruin. Designed to open the door to first-time home buyers with blemished or insubstantial credit histories, subprime loans have helped millions of borrowers purchase homes they might not have been able to purchase otherwise. Subprime loans are considered risky, however, so borrowers pay higher interest rates. These loans often start out with low introductory interest rates—"teasers"—that later escalate.

> **SUBPRIME LOANS:**
> High-interest-rate loans that are offered to borrowers with flawed credit histories

Subprime loans did create widespread disaster when they were offered to financially unsophisticated consumers (who couldn't keep up with payments) by brokers known in the financial industry as predatory, meaning they were willing to exploit or destroy others for gain.

> **PREDATORY BROKERS AND LENDERS:**
> Unethical mortgage brokers and lenders who target financially unsophisticated home buyers, often with offers of subprime loans

In addition to home buyers, these financial predators pursued home owners who wanted to repay credit card and other debts by refinancing their homes. Standards become so dangerously loose that loans were approved for borrowers who were three months late on their current mortgages, or who had filed for bankruptcy or were facing foreclosure on their properties.

Predatory brokers and lenders concentrated their efforts in

neighborhoods that were largely black or Hispanic or both. In 2006, African Americans were 2.3 times more likely and Hispanics twice as likely as whites to get high-cost loans, according to an analysis of loans that were reported under the Home Mortgage Disclosure Act. This didn't happen by accident; predatory lenders targeted blacks and Hispanics.

When researchers from New York University's Furman Center for Real Estate and Urban Policy compared New York City black and Hispanic neighborhoods with white areas where the residents had similar income levels, the ten neighborhoods with the highest rates of mortgages from subprime lenders were found to have minority populations. Even when median income levels were comparable, home owners in neighborhoods with black or Hispanic majorities were more likely than whites to get subprime loans.

Ted Janusz, author of the tell-all book *Kickback: Confessions of a Mortgage Broker* (Insight, 2005), explains that he looked for naïve consumers with flawed credit histories. He and other brokers lured people in by promising a relatively low interest rate, then they jacked up the numbers later. Subprime loans generated enormous profits for the brokers and lending institutions through the high commissions borrowers were charged, often tens of thousands each in additional fees. There was great incentive for local financial institutions to approve as many loans as possible, and with little concern for whether the borrowers would be able to repay.

Undocumented mortgages could not have met the standards of the government institutions Freddie Mac and Fannie Mae, but there were plenty of private well-established firms interested. They made huge commissions and fees, rolling hundreds of millions of dollars in loans, subprime and others, into mortgage-related securities that could be traded like regular bonds and offered to marquee clients.

There was so much profit to be made that many financial institutions also invested their own capital. The securities were considered risky, but historically, only a small percentage of people had defaulted on home loans. Ordinarily, wiser heads might have prevailed. A Federal Reserve governor had warned years earlier that predatory lenders were luring people into risky mortgages that they couldn't afford, and in 2004, housing-advocacy leaders spoke to the head of the Federal Reserve, Alan Greenspan, about the spread of unscrupulous practices. But insane greed ruled the day. There was potential for a high rate of return, a stream of income from little people locked into adjustable-rate mortgage payments that could only go up, and they did: from 7 to 9 percent in the first two or three years to as high as 15 percent.

At some point the bubble had to burst, and it did. Home values fell, right around the time that rising payments on adjustable mortgages came due. Mired in debt, millions of people were unable to keep up their payments. In 2007, the number of home owners who fell dangerously behind in mortgage payments or whose homes went into foreclosure hit record highs, according to the Mortgage Bankers Association. Foreclosures rose to almost 2 million in 2007, up from 1.2 million a year earlier. With money from near and far invested in mortgage-backed securities, and major insurers left holding the bag on more than $1 trillion worth of bonds, financial tremors were felt around the world.

There are lessons to be learned from this mortgage meltdown. As African Americans, we would do well to ensure that our history of being denied home ownership doesn't lead us to indiscriminate eagerness to fulfill what can be a worthy goal.

It's not surprising that so many of us value real estate above other investments. Our enslaved ancestors learned early on that they who owned the land controlled their lives. After the Civil War, former captives experienced crushing disappointment when the federal government failed to make good on the "forty acres and a mule" promise of seizing land from Confederates to sell or give to freedmen.

Half a century later, racist home-loan policies made a lasting impact on African American lives. In the mid-1930s, during the introduction of the New Deal, the Federal Housing Administration (FHA) began offering mortgage assistance by insuring loans made by private lenders. The FHA program offered whites opportunities to start building wealth, but it discriminated blatantly against African Americans. This was the period that ushered in redlining—the practice by lending institutions of denying loans on properties in black neighborhoods. The term *redlining* originated when federal maps were drawn, supposedly indicating which residential areas offered secure real estate investments. These maps bore red outlines around black neighborhoods, which were deemed ineligible for loans. Of course you know that black people weren't welcome in white neighborhoods either. For several decades most African Americans living in urban communities were unable to secure fair-interest loans for new investments, and their properties often deteriorated and lost value. Redlining was successfully challenged in the 1970s, but it is often cited as a factor in residential segregation and urban decay.

> REDLINING:
> The illegal practice of refusing to make mortgage loans in certain areas, which has impacted African American neighborhoods and rates of black home ownership

That's not the end of the story. Although more than one million African Americans served in World War II, most who made it back to the States were unable to take advantage of wealth opportunities that benefited their white counterparts. GI Bill benefits are credited with elevating a generation of white working-class World War II vets who were able to purchase their first homes. In fact, so many homes were sold to returning soldiers that GI Bill benefits fueled a housing boom. It was a different story for African Americans. Compared with whites, African Americans by and large did not benefit from housing assistance provided by the GI Bill, because local bank officials often denied them mortgage loans.

Home ownership has been the principal means by which Americans have acquired wealth. When we were excluded from home ownership, we were also excluded from the most significant opportunity to prosper.

From 1973 to 1978 tens of millions of Americans—the majority of them white—have benefited from suburban home-equity gains. Wealth accumulation through equity allowed many home owners to send their children to college, provide for comfortable retirements, and pass inheritances on to future generations. Real estate equity is calculated by subtracting the mortgage balance from the market value of a piece of property. For instance, someone might buy a house for $150,000. Over a period of ten years, prices in the neighborhood increase, and the home owner has paid off $20,000 of the mortgage and still owes $130,000. The house is now valued at $200,000, so the home owner would have $70,000 in equity. On the other hand, if the value of the property declines, the home owner might wind up owing more than the house is worth.

REAL ESTATE EQUITY:
The difference between what is owed on a property and its value

Through much of the nineties and into the new millennium, housing prices soared. But keep in mind that home values are arbitrary and climb as high or decline as low as the market dictates. For instance, during the eighties it might have been possible to purchase an inexpensive house in an urban neighborhood that many considered undesirable. A decade later, as workers begin to disdain long commutes and search for properties closer to urban centers, the value of that property might rise and so would the equity. Gambling on continued low interest rates and increases in real estate equity, millions of home owners cashed out their equity by taking out loans.

Because fewer African Americans own property and other assets that can be borrowed against, there has been a greater reliance on credit cards and loan companies in the face of emergencies. For too many this has meant tapping into the higher-interest rates of unsecured debt, which negatively impacts credit scores and makes it more difficult to get home loans. African American credit card debt is rising faster than our incomes, causing too many of us to miss out on opportunities for buying homes, investing, and saving.

I often see studies comparing white and black wealth, which inevitably point out that African Americans lag far behind. These reports seldom offer historical explanations as to why this is the case. Now you know that there is far more to the wealth-accumulation race gap than meets the eye. And you also know that history cannot defeat us; we can only defeat ourselves.

I believe that the events that kept many African Americans locked out of the housing market have a very different tone from the discriminatory acts that came to light in 2007. Some community activists are correct in charging that during the subprime crisis banks practiced "reverse redlining," by targeting black borrowers for unfair credit terms. An estimated 15 to 50 percent of the subprime loans purchased by Freddie Mac and Fannie Mae in 2005 went to borrowers whose credit scores indicated that they could have qualified for prime loans. Predatory brokers clearly realized they could earn higher fees with subprime mortgages. They were betting that these home owners would be financially illiterate and wouldn't know to demand the mortgage rates they deserved. The losses these hardworking people incurred are telling examples of the old saying "What you don't know *can* hurt you."

In the past, our people were made to feel powerless; that changed when civil rights champions led a movement to end legal discrimination. Today, although racism lingers, we have another tool at the ready: financial literacy. When used correctly, it is as powerful as the forces that shook America and forced open gates of opportunity.

That's why I told Ms. Brooks, and why I say to you unequivocally, despite the experiences reported during the subprime meltdown, if you're dreaming of buying a place of your own and you've learned how to make home ownership work to your financial advantage, go for it. It is still one of the best opportunities for building wealth and economic security.

Ms. Brooks did buy her home. She couldn't have looked more satisfied on the day she invited friends and family to join her and her pastor for a house-blessing ceremony. She learned that buying a house is no easy feat but that there are numerous benefits to ownership. The primary benefit is that over time, as you pay down your balance, your equity grows. And home ownership lightens your tax burden. The government allows home owners to deduct part of their mortgage interest and real estate taxes. There are psychological benefits as well. Home ownership can help you feel invested in a community. In surveys, people rank home ownership as second only to health in terms of qualities that foster happiness.

But I urge you *not* to think of your home as your primary retirement strategy. As you have seen, there might be a time when your house won't be worth as much as you'd like or when it will be difficult to sell at a profit. Untold numbers of people who took out subprime loans against their homes were forced into foreclosure when they were unable to meet the high payments. When factoring your retirement needs, please consider real estate as one option among several.

INVESTING IN RESIDENTIAL PROPERTIES TO PREPARE FOR RETIREMENT

Taking our history into account can help separate your desire to own from the practicality of home ownership. In keeping with all that we have reviewed in this chapter, it's important to raise the subject of investing in rental properties in preparation for retirement. At least 10 percent of my clients own rental real estate. I often encourage investing in residential properties as long as you:

1. Have liquid money available for emergencies.

2. Aren't putting all of your eggs in one basket, by which I mean your assets are diversified, lessening your degree of risk.

3. Have the time to maintain the property as well as respond to tenants' needs and the other obligations involved in being a landlord.

4. Become thoroughly educated on the subject of real estate by attending seminars and workshops, discussing the ins and outs with pros, and reading up on the subject. (There are numerous guides available. I suggest browsing through titles at your local bookstore or online at Amazon.com.)

The greatest benefit of investing in rental real estate with retirement in mind is that if the property is maintained, it can appreciate year after year. Whether you have one or multiple tenants over the years, their rent payments help to pay off the mortgage as the property increases in value. Over time, as prices rise, you're able to charge higher rents, and after the property is paid off and overhead costs are met, you have regular money coming in to supplement your income—which is another form of annuity.

Whether you're interested in home ownership, investing in rental properties, or both, the focus on real estate continues in the next chapter, which was designed to help you consider what's best for you when it comes to renting, owning a home, or borrowing on one that you already own when factoring in your retirement needs.

HELPFUL HINT

Learn how to avoid mortgage fraud and get other useful information on buying a house or getting a home loan by attending free or low-cost education courses offered by the U.S. Department of Housing and Urban Development. To register for a class in your area, call toll-free at (800) 569-4287 or go online to www .hud.gov/offices/hsg/sfh/buying/loanfraud.cfm.

BUILDING FINANCIAL LITERACY

The word *recession* refers to a period of two quarters or more of slowed national economic activity. There's no consensus on what causes a recession, but it is characterized by a gathering force of trends that can include rising unemployment and oil prices and downturns in consumer spending, trade, investing, and industrial output. During a recession it can be harder to get a job, loans are more difficult to secure, and lending standards become stricter. When the economy slows significantly, government leaders might try to avert or ease recessions by putting more money into the hands of Americans through tax cuts and rebates, temporary increases in unemployment benefits, and increased government spending on infrastructure, such as highways and bridges. The head of the Federal Reserve—a group of banks that regulate the nation's money supply—may lower interest rates. Inflation—the upward movement of the prices of goods and services—can rise during a recession. But generally, when the economy slows, the demand for goods and services is reduced. No one can change the fundamental dynamics of the economy, but if you're in the black—living within your means and paying yourself whether the nation's financial climate is bright or gloomy—you're more likely to prosper.

> RECESSION:
> A period of two quarters or more marking a slowdown in national economic activity

CONSIDERING SCRIPTURE

"Therefore may it please you to bless the house of your servant, that it may continue forever before you. For you, O Lord, have blessed and are blessed forever."

—I Chronicles 17:27.

If the spirit moves you, read this passage aloud and write about its meaning as you become more financially literate.

_____

_____

_____

_____

_____

14

Knowing Whether to Rent or Buy, Stay or Downsize or Relocate

This chapter is designed to help you decide, based upon your financial situation and your retirement plans, whether you should continue renting, purchase your first home, or stay in the home you may own. While you're welcome to read all three sections, you might want to choose the one that is most pertinent to your current situation.

IF YOU'RE RENTING, DON'T GIVE UP ON YOUR DREAMS OF BUYING

Calvin Bentley, sixty-two, a Jaguar salesman in Atlanta, Georgia, wished he had settled down long enough to develop equity in a house. "I'm single and I love traveling. My job has given me opportunities to live in London, Scotland, Rome, Madrid, Tokyo, and Lagos." Through all of these relocations, he has maintained an elegant penthouse apartment in Atlanta, paying about $3,500 a month. "It's easy enough for me to pay now, but the rent is bound to go up, so who knows what it will be in 2028 when I'm eighty."

In the end, Mr. Bentley bit the bullet, staying at his job five years longer than he had planned, reducing his expenses and adding to his savings by cutting back on travel. Then he purchased an elegant condo for $357,000.

If you're renting and trying to decide whether you can afford to buy a home before you retire, consider these points:

- **Maintaining good credit scores can save you thousands on a mortgage.** There's a saying that is especially apropos here: What you earn determines your lifestyle, but your credit score determines your wealth. When it comes to buying a home and you need to improve your financial profile, aim for a low debt-to-income ratio, which simply means that you don't have a lot of your money tied up in unsecured debt. Mortgage brokers will scour details of your payment history in your credit report and determine the amount you can borrow, in large part on the basis of your score. To find out how your FICO score (credit score) will impact the interest rate you pay on a loan, use the loan calculator online at www.myfico.com/myfico/CreditCentral/LoanRates.asp.

- **Hang on to your job.** You may want to work a few more years than you've planned. Steady employment and a credit history that includes working for the same employer or in the same line of work for two or more years are highly valued by mortgage lenders.

- **Downsizing, getting a roommate, or moving to a less expensive area can help you save.** You might feel you're at an age where you don't want to inconvenience yourself with a move or a roommate, but if you're paying high rent, these options will lower your expenses.

- **Purchasing a home can lower your tax liability.** That's something that might be helpful, depending on your postretirement income. Those with substantial postretirement incomes may benefit from deducting mortgage interest, home-equity debt, and real estate taxes from their income taxes. Talk with a financial professional before making a decision. Or go online to find out whether purchasing a house can lower your tax bill. Plug your information in to the easy buying-versus-renting calculator, available online at www.ginniemae.gov/rent_vs_buy/rent_vs_buy_calc.asp?Section=YPTH. You can also consult a tax professional or call the IRS telephone assistance line at (800) 829-1040.

- **You might want to relocate after retiring.** Since homes cost so much to buy and maintain, if you're retiring anytime soon and plan to change locations within the next two years, you might be better off renting for now. It costs a great deal not only to get into a house but to sell it as well, which means a short stay could cause you to lose money.

- **If you do plan to relocate and downsize, compare home prices and the rental market in your prospective area.** Some locales are rich in low-cost rentals but have hugely inflated real estate stock. If you're not planning to sell a home and pay cash on a new one, once you get prequalified (see below) and have an idea of how much you can expect to pay monthly on a mortgage, figure out the difference between that and rental prices. When calculating costs for your retirement planning, remember that home owners pay real estate taxes and insurance and are responsible for landscaping, painting, yard upkeep, appliances, and repairs on the roof, boiler, structures, plumbing, electrical, heating, and sewage systems.

- **Getting prequalified will give you a reality check.** Prequalification is an informal, usually free process that helps a lender or a Realtor look at your income and expenses and calculate your debt-to-income ratio. Once you're prequalified, you'll have a ballpark figure of the price range you can afford, and from this point on you might want to attend open houses to see what your money can buy. You already have your financial documents organized, and that will be quite helpful here. I've included a checklist of the documents you'll want to take along with you to get the prequalification ball rolling.

  ❏ **Two months of pay stubs**
  ❏ **Two years of W-2 forms**
  ❏ **Debt and bank information**
  ❏ **Proof of any other income**

PREQUALIFICATION:
A nonbinding process involving a lender or a Realtor to establish how much house you can afford

If you haven't yet established a long credit history, you can also bring canceled checks showing regularly scheduled payments on your rent and various utilities, as well as canceled checks showing that you're repaying a student loan as agreed.

- **Starting a housing fund will work to your advantage.** Even if you've made some credit mistakes, lenders will look at you more favorably if you demonstrate consistent patterns of saving. If you're a first-time buyer, you might find it difficult to secure a house with a zero down-payment option. Down payments range anywhere from 5 to 20 percent of the sale price on a house, and you will also have to pay closing costs. (See "If You're a First-Time Buyer" on page 201 for details.)

You'll also be required to demonstrate that you have reserve funds that can tide you over for a few months during rough times. After prequalification, you'll have a better idea how much you'll need to save. Once you come up with a figure, set a target date, and don't forget the power of visualization. Take photos of houses that strike your fancy, or cut pictures from a magazine and tape at least one to your bathroom mirror and inside your journal or this book to remind you to keep working toward your goal.

If you don't have equity from the sale of a home when you're relocating, you might want to fund a housing account by securing extra work and declaring a moratorium on buying gadgets, clothes, or whatever might lead to overspending. Some people use the enthusiasm generated when they start saving for a down payment as motivation to cut back on expensive habits, such as smoking, buying fast food, or going to bars. Collaborative personalities might enjoy organizing friends who are also determined to buy property, so you can meet regularly and share savings strategies.

- **You might qualify for a down-payment aid program.** Some nonprofit agencies offer down-payment aid to help needy families buy their first homes. These programs can be found on the Web, but don't confuse them with commercial down-payment assistance loans, which have to be repaid, usually at high interest. Down-payment aid programs will actually *give* you money. Two established nonprofit down-payment aid programs can be found online at www.ameridream.org and www.getdownpayment.com.

- **You might qualify for FHA loan.** Retirement might give you more time to work on a fixer-upper. If you're buying your first home or a fixer-upper and qualify for a Federal Housing Authority loan, your down payment could be a low percentage of the purchase price, and most of your closing costs and fees could be included in the loan. The program is designed to help low- to moderate-income families purchase their first home. Here are the requirements for FHA loans:

1. Two years of steady employment, preferably with the same employer

2. Steady income that has increased in the last two years or at least remained the same

3. A credit report with no more than two 30-day-late payments in the last two years

4. Bankruptcy that is at least two years in the past, followed by good credit

5. Foreclosure that is three years in the past, followed by good credit

6. Mortgage payments that will represent no more than 30 percent of your gross income

For more information, call (800) 569-4287 or go online to www.hud.gov/buying/loans.cfm.

IF YOU'RE A FIRST-TIME BUYER

Benita Morgan was beside herself with joy. "Praise the Lord," she said. I understood why she was ecstatic. For four decades she'd dedicated her life to raising her five children in a Chicago housing project, working two jobs to keep food on the table and help them pay for college tuition. She had insisted that all five of her kids attend college. With the last one graduated and employed, they gathered together on Mother's Day 2003 to share something that they'd been hiding from her.

She already knew this would be their last dinner together in their run-down Chicago apartment, because Miss Morgan planned to relocate to Hampton, Virginia, to take care of her elderly mother. One aspect of her plan had been altered, however. She and her mother wouldn't be moving to a rented house. Her kids had pooled $27,000, enough for her to make a down payment on a new brick home, pay closing costs, and bank $5,000 as a cushion. They had done their job in finding out what was entailed in first-time home buying. Following are tips for anyone who's buying for the first time or selling and relocating:

Consider buying a condominium

Since they require less maintenance, this might be just the ticket as you grow older. Although condos are often sold at lower prices than single-family homes, they offer the same tax advantages.

Check out property taxes

These vary widely from state to state and from city to city, so before you buy you'll want to find areas that are affordable.

When choosing a home, factor in your present and future needs

The goal for most seniors is to remain independent for as long as possible, so choose your new place with aging in mind. For instance, if you're looking at a condo that is not located on the ground floor, make sure the building has a reliable elevator. Parking should be conveniently located, and you'll want something close to public transportation and a short distance to medical facilities and doctors. Whether they live in a house or apartment, many of my clients are happier residing close to family members or longtime friends. It can be isolating to move to a new town, where you have few ties. With that in mind, if you're moving to a new city or state, you will want to look for a location where the greater community shares your values, and it almost goes without saying that you'll want to settle in a neighborhood that feels welcoming.

Seek Realtor recommendations from folks you know

People who've already purchased their own homes will be more than willing to share the names of Realtors who helped them buy a house.

Ask questions about whose interests the agent will represent, and hold out for someone who you feel is in your corner and not the seller's.

Get preapproved

This is a formal process through which you seek a commitment from financial institutions to lend you money if you buy a house. You'll be asked to fill out a mortgage application. Make sure you go to at least three financial institutions, rather than independent brokers (who often have no oversight), so you can compare interest rates and estimates of closing fees. Start with the institution where you do your banking. Since you already have a history there, you might receive favorable rates. Once you get offers, ask brokers for advice about what you can do to lower your interest rate. Your resulting preapproval information can be used when you're narrowing in on a property and you want to demonstrate that the loan will be approved if you make an offer. Because a show of inquiries from lenders will affect your credit score negatively, it's best to make copies of your credit report to give lenders. Your goal here is to get a prequalification letter or, even better, a preapproval letter from your chosen lender. Your Realtor will need to present this letter to a seller when she makes an offer to purchase a property on your behalf.

> PREAPPROVAL:
> This process requires filling out a mortgage application to qualify for a loan. Once you're preapproved, the lender commits to a maximum mortgage amount and an interest rate.

Consider applying for a mortgage loan through a credit union, where you are likely to be treated personally. If you don't belong to a credit union or have access to one, ask relatives who might. All you need to qualify for a credit union membership is a family connection.

Ask lenders for "good-faith" estimates

The government requires lenders to mail you this disclosure form no more than three days after you've applied for the loan. It lists estimates of all your closing costs. Lenders may omit some fees in this estimate in an attempt to make their offers look favorable. Compare fees on at least three estimates.

> **GOOD-FAITH ESTIMATE:**
> A lender's summary of estimated costs for a mortgage

Some origination fees—charges from lenders for processing a loan application—can be as much as 5 percent on a commission, which could mean a $10,000 commission on a $200,000 loan. Negotiate for lower terms, or insist that the fee be dropped entirely. Some closing fees are negotiable. And remember to compare this estimate to the fees listed on the good-faith estimate so you can make certain that your lender hasn't packed the loan with additional fees in the fine print.

Learn about the differences in loan options

Terms can run from five to thirty years. Here are some of the most popular types of mortgages:

- **Fixed mortgages.** These are traditional loans in which the interest rate remains unchanged. They offer stability and long-term tax advantages, since they usually involve thirty-year terms.

- **Adjustable-rate mortgages (ARMs).** Interest rates change from month to month, depending on changes in the prime rate (the rate that banks advertise as their best loan rate) or other indexes, which the loan uses as its reference point. ARMs have a ceiling that can be reset each year. These are the type of loans that led to so many defaults. ARMs don't necessarily cause disaster, especially for someone who can count on a big income increase in the near future. Still, the borrower should be aware that although ARMs might start out at relatively low rates, they can rise steeply.

- **Pay-option adjustable-rate mortgages.** This is another of the mortgages implicated in the subprime scandal. It seems particularly attractive because its low introductory rate allows borrowers to pay even less than the interest due. The difference is added onto the balance, which means that more is owed with each passing month.

- **Balloon mortgages.** Imagine a balloon starting out as a flat piece of rubber and then growing enormous, and you've got the picture on this kind of loan. These are structured over a short term, starting out with a fixed rate and, at the end of five to seven years, requiring that the outstanding balance be paid in one lump sum, either by refinancing or out of pocket.

- **Biweekly mortgages.** For the borrower who wants to pay off the loan at a faster pace, this fixed-rate mortgage might be the ticket. This type of mortgage has to be paid every two weeks. You can find more information on paying off mortgages early under "If You Own Your Own Home," on page 208.

- **80-10-10 mortgage.** This is also known as a "piggy-back" loan. You pay 10 percent down and take out two loans—one for 80 percent, the other for the remaining 10 percent. This works for someone who can afford to pay off the second loan fairly soon, for it will reduce the total payment. Those who can't afford to pay off the second loan within a year or so should be aware that interest rates on second mortgages are generally 2 percent higher and the term is shorter than the main mortgage, usually fifteen years instead of thirty.

All of the loans described might include a nonrecourse feature, which means that the lender will use the purchased property—and only that property—as security. If the borrower defaults, the lender is entitled only to the property. But policies vary from state to state, so before you buy a home, you'll want to check whether lenders in your state can seize your other assets, should you become unable to meet the terms of your mortgage.

If you or your spouse served in the military, apply for a veteran's home loan

Backed by the federal government, these loans allow you to buy a house with no down payment.

Consult a real estate attorney or HUD-certified housing counselor before you sign

If you can afford hourly fees, seek guidance from a real estate attorney, who will explain the fine print, such as prepenalty fees (in which the lender charges you for paying off your loan early—a stipulation you might want to avoid). Another source of legal advice is a Department of Housing and Urban Development (HUD)–certified counseling agency, which is free of charge or low cost. For information on finding an agency near you, go online to www.hud .gov/offices/hsg/sfh/hcc/hcs.cfm?webListAction=search&search state=IL.

Pay attention to the interest rates you're offered

You've already learned about compound interest, so you won't be surprised to see the difference between what two people might pay on a thirty-year mortgage for a $250,000 house. At 6.108 percent interest, monthly payments will come to $1,516.28, with a total interest of $295,860 over the life of the loan. For someone charged 7.921 percent interest on the same $250,000 loan, monthly payments will be $1,821, with total interest of $405,437 over the life of the loan. The difference is more than $100,000. Your interest rate will be tied to your credit score, so consider whether you need to take more time to improve yours. To take a look at prevailing interest rates, visit www.hsh.com.

Understand points

You can reduce the cost of your interest rate by purchasing points, prepaid interest fees. Those running low on cash can choose a zero-point option, but as you know, the lower your interest, the more you save in the long run, so buy points if possible. If the seller seems anxious to sell the house, you can ask him to buy down your points.

POINTS:
Fees that enable buyers to buy down their interest rates. A point is worth 1 percent of the loan amount.

Know your annual percentage rate

This is the annual cost of a loan, including interest, insurance, and the origination fee (points), expressed as a percentage.

Be prepared to pay closing costs

You received a good-faith estimate, and now you find that the fees are higher than originally estimated. Closing costs can be as much as 5 percent of what you're paying for the house and mortgage, mortgage application, and house-inspection fees.

Be prepared to pay property taxes and home owner's insurance

Rather than using your lender to contract this for you at inflated prices, consider going to an insurance company for more favorable prices. You will be required to pay one year up front.

Keep copies of your deed of trust and all mortgage paperwork

In addition to adding the original to your documents file, make a copy and give it to your attorney or a loved one for safekeeping.

IF YOU OWN YOUR OWN HOME

Dr. Geri Lanier, sixty-four, a Nevada psychologist, was anxious to join her husband in Maryland. The two had been married for forty-three years and had never been apart until he had retired a year ahead of her and moved to Maryland, planning to build their dream house. They'd purchased property in 2005 and were about to break ground in 2007, when the mortgage meltdown brought everything to a halt. They'd planned to list their home for $420,000 and use the proceeds to help pay for their half-million-dollar dream house. But the value of their house had dropped 33 percent, and she was finding it next to impossible to sell, even at a steep discount.

Her husband wanted to sell off a chunk of their sizable invest-ments and go ahead with their building plans, but she insisted on getting professional advice first. They began working with me at the recommendation of one of my clients. I suggested that it would work to their advantage to sell one house before they started the new one, so they wouldn't be carrying two mortgages at once. I further explained that losses in the housing sector had also driven down the value of their investment portfolio, and that it was not wise to sell stocks at a loss for the purpose of building a new house. Mr. Lanier was disappointed that his wife wanted to post-pone plans on their new house, but he agreed. They rented out their Nevada home—after hiring a property manager—and kept it on the market. Dr. Lanier retired and joined her husband in Mary-land, where they settled temporarily into a rental a few miles from their property. This way, they could get to know their new com-munity and establish a home base that would allow them to keep a close eye on the house construction once it began.

If you're a home owner planning for retirement, here are some other considerations to keep in mind:

Don't view your home as a bank

The Laniers wisely planned to use the equity in one house to fi-nance another. Home owners should always curb any tendency to think of the equity in their house as a source of funds for paying off unsecured debt. And you won't want to overrely on your house to finance your retirement. If you plan to live in it, you'll need other sources of income to keep you going. Besides, if prices drop, you could lose the net worth as your equity erodes.

Apply for a home-equity line of credit (HELOC)

After reading horror stories about people who borrowed money against their homes and then lost them through foreclosure, you might feel hesitant to consider this. But let me explain how to use a home-equity line of credit to your advantage. Once your application is approved, you never have to use the money in this account, and it won't cost you a dime to have it in place. But should you (or any other breadwinner you depend on) lose a job or experience any interruption in income, you can draw down on your HELOC funds and continue making mortgage payments until you come up with another source of income. This way, you won't have to worry about falling behind on your mortgage. If you do draw down on your HELOC, make every effort to pay it off as quickly as possible.

Pay off your mortgage early

To fight the interest compounding on your loan, pay half of your typical monthly mortgage payment every two weeks, rather than once a month. This way, you will greatly speed up the payoff of the loan. It's half of what you would pay anyway, so it's not likely to adversely affect your budget. You can find a biweekly mortgage calendar online at www.bankrate.com/brm/cgi-bin/biweekly.asp. If you're worried about forgetting to send the checks twice each month, set up biweekly automatic payments. Before you decide to do this, however, check to see whether your mortgage includes a prepenalty fee stipulation, allowing the lender to charge you for paying off your loan early. If it does, call the lender and ask how that charge will translate, then decide whether you're willing to pay it anyway for the sake of peace of mind.

If you're having difficulty making your mortgage payment

1. Call your lender to see whether you can convince a loan officer to agree to a plan that will avoid further delinquency.

2. Contact a local HUD-approved counseling agency and make an appointment with an adviser who can help you come up with an action plan for saving your house. For the telephone numbers and addresses of HUD-approved counseling agencies, go online and Google "HUD approved housing counseling agencies."

3. Contact the Homeownership Preservation Foundation, a free credit-counseling service, at (888) 995-HOPE (4673).

A reverse mortgage

You may not like the idea of placing another mortgage on your home and you also might want to bequeath your house to family members. But if you desperately need to pay off debt and/or you have no other options to provide for your future, consider a home-equity conversion mortgage (HECM), which is a federally insured reverse mortgage. Depending on the value and condition of your home, a reverse mortgage can get cash flowing. The repayment is not due until the last borrower (if you and a spouse or relative own the home together) leaves. This will allow you to get equity out of your mortgage that you don't have to repay, and if you have beneficiaries, they can decide whether to repay the loan by selling the property. For more information on government-financed reverse mortgages, go online to www.hud.gov/offices/hsg/sfh/hecm/hecmhome.cfm or phone (800) FED-INFO (333-4636). Be sure to consult with a financial counselor before you sign for this option. And just say no to any door-to-door salespeople who might try to pressure you into agreeing to a reverse mortgage, especially if it involves putting the proceeds of the loan into investments that will put your money out of reach. This is not the kind of decision you want to make with a stranger. Please consult a financial professional for advice.

Fluctuations in the housing market underscore the message

that there is no such thing as a guaranteed investment. Some successful investors are lucky, but the smartest ones are well informed.

BUILDING FINANCIAL LITERACY

Real estate investment trusts (REITs) are investments for people who want to own property but don't want to be landlords. REITs sell like stocks to allow for investments on commercial properties and mortgages. They provide commercial space for some of the biggest names in business.* Individuals can invest in REITs either by purchasing shares directly on an open exchange or by investing in a mutual fund that specializes in public real estate.

* Historically, a portfolio that includes REITs tends to be less volatile than those that feature more speculative equities. However, REITs are no guarantee of favorable results and involve investment risks, including loss of principal.

"Hear, O Israel: The Lord is our God, the Lord alone. You shall love the Lord your God with all your heart, and with all your soul, and with all your might. Keep these words that I am commanding you today in your heart. Recite them to your children and talk about them when you are at home and when you are away, when you lie down and when you rise. Bind them as a sign on your hand, fix them as an emblem on your forehead, and write them on the doorposts of your house and on your gates." —Deuteronomy 6:4–9.

If the spirit moves you, read this passage aloud and write about its meaning in your life as you become more financially literate.

_____

_____

_____

_____

_____

_____

_____

STEP 7

Don't Just Play the Market, Understand It

15

Making Wall Street Work for You

Since opening my practice in 1993, I've witnessed a tremendous shift in clients' attitudes about investing in the stock market. People are becoming aware that even if they have never put a dime into the market directly, one way or another they're probably already invested. The funds allocated for pensions and 401(k)-type plans and the dollars earmarked for Social Security accounts aren't locked away in a bank vault. Financial managers invest the money so it will grow before they have to pay it back, and many of those investments are in the stock market.

And then there's personal investing, which eliminates the middleman and creates potential for greater gains on your part, but with greater risks. It is this risk factor that stops a lot of people from investing. Is fear of the unknown holding you back?

Perhaps you keep all your money in a savings account. You may be earning minimal interest, but feel that your risks are minimal because the federal government backs deposits up to $100,000 (that amount has increased to at least $250,000 per depositor, per insured bank, at least through 2009). With personal investing you never know for sure how much you will lose or gain. And withdrawing your money isn't as easy as just showing up when a bank, credit union, or savings and loan opens. For those and other reasons, people tell me that they would never get involved in investing. One man said, "That's why they call it *playing* the stock market. And when it comes to my money, I don't play."

From my point of view, "playing" with money is handing over your hard-earned cash to an institution that makes a big profit by investing it and then pays you a pittance. I'm not opposed to taking the safe route. Everyone should keep money available in a liquid account at a financial institution. And personal investing is not for everyone—after reading this chapter, you'll be able to decide whether it's right for you.

As a financial consultant, my job is not to convince people to invest but to take the fear out of investing so clients can decide whether it is in their best interests. If you're an investor, you already know why it's important to consider this financial tool when planning for the future. Because on the road to retirement you can limp along, as if driving on a spare tire, or you can get your engine turbocharged and put some distance between you and that annoying driver who's tailgating and threatening to run you off the road. You probably know that the annoying "driver" is inflation.

There are few hard-and-fast rules when it comes to investing on your own or through a broker, but there are ways to develop a greater sense of control. You can avoid obsessing over market fluctuations by employing a long-term strategy of only investing money that you can do without for five years or more. That way, when there's a market downturn you can wait for it to rebound so you won't have to sell at a loss.

That brings me to my next point. Whatever money you do invest, remind yourself that there will be years when your earnings will be higher and years when they'll be lower. Investing involves losses as well as gains. You might take comfort in knowing that over time, market gains have traditionally outnumbered market losses by far.

New York University's Stern School of Business found that in the period from 1928 to 2006, stock returns averaged 11.77 percent. That same analysis, focusing on a narrower, more recent window of time, from 1996 to 2006, found that stock market returns averaged 11.06 percent. This suggests that despite economic downturns, when it comes to planning for the future, investing, followed by reinvesting earnings and letting them compound over time, is generally considered the most effective strategy for beating inflation and creating wealth.*

Too many of us are missing out on investment gains. By 2002, 74 percent of high-income African Americans were participating in the market, including 401(k)-type plans, according to an Ariel/ Schwab survey. But those numbers soon eroded, and we don't have to look back far in history to understand why. At the start of the new millennium, from 2000 through 2001, after the dot-com bubble burst, a tide of investors experienced losses. In the years immediately following, the black participation rate dipped to 57 percent. If fear of investing is keeping you out of the market, it might help to know that a range of options exists, allowing you to make choices based on your level of risk tolerance. Brushing up on the investment basics might help raise your comfort level with investing. The explanations that follow are by no means meant to be comprehensive. And while you might come across a few unfamiliar terms initially, I hope you will stick with me.

Let's start by imagining that you and a group of colleagues are undertaking the development and construction of a retirement

---

* This is not a guarantee of favorable results. Investing involves some risks, including loss of principal.

village built close to a historically black college and a major medical facility, in a region of the country that offers low taxes, mild temperatures, and a pastoral setting and yet is only a short distance from a vibrant city. This apartment village would be viewed as a paradise for African American retirees leaving harsher urban environments, with larger units available for families still housing teenagers as well as older relatives. This village will be safe and relatively affordable, beautifully landscaped, with guest apartments available for visiting family members, and will provide opportunities for participating at local churches and volunteering at the neighboring college and public schools.

The building plans for this $30 million project generate lots of excitement. You and other members of your business consortium kick in some of your own cash, form a legal corporation, and attract various government grants. In an effort to raise a final $10 million, you sell bonds and stocks to investors.

Two years later, your dreams have been realized: You have a 90 percent occupancy rate. Here's how you return the money that is owed: All along, bondholders have been receiving regular interest payments from your corporation, and now it's time for them to be repaid the original amount of the loan. At some point, if business continues going well, stockholders will be compensated. This repayment hierarchy is significant when it comes to understanding investment basics.

Perhaps you noticed that the scenario involved three types of investments: cash, bonds, and stocks. Let's discuss them in more detail.

CASH

In this scenario, members of the business consortium contributed some of their own cash toward the development of the retirement village. Perhaps some of them dipped into their savings. Consider your own situation concerning cash. Where do you keep money that you might need either for emergencies or for meeting short-term goals, such as a down payment on a car or house? It's advisable to keep at least six months worth of salary in a money market or savings account. Certificates of deposit, which are also considered "cash" accounts, generally offer higher yields because the financial institution holds on to your money for an agreed-upon period.

BONDS

In raising money for your retirement village, you issued bonds—debt instruments that are like IOUs issued for the purpose of raising capital. Entities that issue bonds promise to repay the loan on a specified date. They essentially say, "Lend us money and we'll repay you with interest."

> **BONDS:**
> IOUs issued by governments or corporate entities for the purpose of raising capital

Federal, state, and local governments, corporations, and other institutions issue (sell) bonds. Bondholders are creditors. In buying a bond that is backed by a government or insurance company, you're making a secured loan. The risk of a bond is a measure of how likely the issuer is considered to be able to fully repay bondholders. Bonds are generally considered good investments for building retirement wealth because they are designed to pay fixed interest regularly—an amount agreed upon at the time of the sale. Dependable interest payments might make bond buying relatively easy on the blood pressure, but bond yields tend to be lower than those of stocks. A rule of thumb in investing is the lower the risk, the lower the return. Although bonds are considered less risky than stocks, they, too, hold a degree of risk.*

Types of Bonds

Credit risk is not the only risk faced by bondholders. For example, some bonds are "callable," which means if interest rates decline, the issuer can call them back in. Investors are then paid the interest due up to that point as well as the amount of the original investment. The bonds are resold at a lower rate. For a more detailed description of risk factors, visit www.investinginbonds.com.

GOVERNMENT BONDS: The money collected by federal, state, and local governments in taxes isn't sufficient for funding what is actually spent. Governments sell bonds to finance everything from highways, bridges, and rail systems to sewers and levees. Bonds sold by the U.S. government are referred to as Treasuries, and those from state or local governments are municipals or munis.

- **Municipal bonds.** The State of New York sold bonds to finance rebuilding Ground Zero after the 2001 terrorist attacks. The yields on these munis were tax-free to New York residents. Munis can be popular with investors who are residents of the states in which the bonds are issued because the yields are often exempt from federal, state, and local taxes.

- **Treasury bonds.** If you've ever received or given someone a U.S. savings bond, one form of federal-government bonds, you probably felt confident that the government

---

*Bonds involve a degree of risk due to interest rates, credit, and inflation. Long-term bonds have more exposure to interest-rate risk than short-term bonds. Lower-rated bonds might offer higher yields in return for more credit risk.

was good for the money. That sense of reliability is one of the major attractions for people who buy and sell another type of Treasury bonds, those that are marketable. Yields from these federal bonds are exempt from state and local taxes but subject to federal taxes.

CORPORATE BONDS: These tend to carry a somewhat higher risk and therefore offer a higher rate of return. Commercial bonds are sold by companies, such as IBM or Google, and are issued with different alphabetical ratings, as determined by independent third-party ratings agencies, such as Standard & Poor's or Moody's. Triple-A is the highest level of bond that's offered. The payout date can be a year, six years, or longer. You can also buy bonds from companies offering triple-B bonds, all the way down to triple-D. High-yield and "junk bonds" are also available. They are ranked low, indicating that they have a relatively high risk of default and offer higher returns.

STOCKS

While bondholders are creditors, stock investors essentially become corporate owners, and they are entitled to a share of the profits—after bondholders are paid. Only corporations can issue stocks. While stocks carry the greatest risks, they also have the potential for the greatest returns—which explains why investors take the risk. Picture a pie that is sliced into equal portions, and you get the idea. There are a finite number of shares in each corporation, so when demand increases, the price of a company's stock rises. But let's say news gets around that a product is defective. For example, a real estate downturn might cause panic among those who invested in our fictional retirement village. They worry about predictions that millions of retiring baby boomers will have trouble selling their homes and will therefore not be able to afford to buy retirement properties. Some investors in the retirement village might sell their stock.

If a great many investors sell, the value of the stock might decline. Some investors might hold on to their stock and wait to see if the price rebounds. The perceived risk of a particular stock is based in part on a company's track record. A lower stock risk is generally associated with larger companies with established histories of paying a portion of the company's earnings to shareholders. These profits are called dividends. Companies considered the most financially reliable and that are known for selling quality products and generating profits during economically challenging times issue what is called "blue-chip" stocks, which are considered to have less risk than many other kinds of stocks.

Mutual Funds

In addition to buying stocks individually, you can purchase them in packages (portfolios) known as mutual funds. When you invest in a mutual fund, you're buying stocks in a variety of companies. The word *mutual* refers to something shared by two or more individuals. Mutual-fund managers pool the deposits of many investors. Picture several companies inside a bubble—offering a diverse mix that might include, for example, companies that specialize in energy, real estate, health, retail, and the financial sectors—and you've got the idea.

One type of mutual fund, an index fund, is a specific group of stocks that are chosen to match the performance of the stock market. The S&P index, a type of index fund, is maintained by Standard & Poor's, the company that monitors a list of five hundred of the largest U.S. companies.

The diversification offered by a mutual fund can work to the investor's advantage. One sector might be going through a downturn (real estate, for example), while another sector, such as health care, is enjoying a banner year, offsetting losses. Some mutual funds specialize in one sector, such as energy, health, or retail.

You might already know that the stock market* isn't a supermarket but a location where buyers and sellers communicate about the trading of stocks and shares by entities such as the New York Stock Exchange (NYSE), the National Association of Securities Dealers Automated Quotation System (NASDAQ), and the American Stock Exchange (AMEX).

Activity on the stock market is said to go up or down. This analysis depends on the Dow Jones Industrial Average, which

---

* Investing in the stock market through individual stocks or mutual funds involves risks, including possible loss of principal. Please consider your risk tolerance carefully and consult a professional adviser before investing.

measures price variations among the thirty most notable blue-chip U.S. stocks, including Microsoft and Home Depot. There are also U.S. regional stock exchanges. If you saw the film or read the book *The Pursuit of Happyness*, you might recall that financial executive Chris Gardner is associated with the Pacific Stock Exchange in San Francisco. Stock exchanges are located in various cities around the world, including Shanghai and London.

I hope that learning the basics has helped to take some of the mystery out of investing. You can expand your knowledge by watching financial-news shows, reading the *Wall Street Journal*, the business section of your daily newspaper, and monthly magazines such as *Black Enterprise*, *Kiplinger's Personal Finance*, and *Money*.

IF YOU DECIDE TO INVEST

The more familiar you become with investing, the more likely you are to devise strategies that fit your needs and level of risk tolerance. Here are a few guidelines:

- **Keep your portfolio diversified.** This helps reduce risk and the possibility of volatile returns. The idea is to make different kinds of investments, some that are short-term, others in stocks, bonds, et cetera. You don't want to keep all your eggs in one basket.

- **Avoid extremes.** Investors lose when they get too fearful or greedy. Greed may lead an investor to put money into what someone describes as a "sure bet." There are no sure bets in investing, unless someone is involved in insider trading, which is illegal. And someone who is too fearful may stick to all low-risk investments, which might make it difficult to keep pace with inflation.

- **Don't overinvest in a company, including your own.** That's what many employees did at Enron, a leading energy company in Houston. Some invested their life savings in Enron stock and then lost everything when the company declared bankruptcy because of fraud by top managers. Most experts advise that your portfolio should not include more than 10 percent of your employer's stock—or of any other investment, for that matter.

- **Hire a retirement professional familiar with investments.** At the end of this book you will find tips on interviewing financial consultants.

- **Take your age into consideration.** If you have thirty to forty years to go before retiring, you can afford to take more risk than someone sixty-five or older who will need to start relying on a nest egg in the near future and won't have as much time to recover from errors. Some people follow this rule of thumb: Take the number 100 and subtract your age. If you're sixty, you should consider having 60 percent of your investments in bonds and 40 percent in stocks. The highest number goes into bonds, so that the older you get, the more bonds you have in your portfolio. That's only one concept to consider. You'll want to make decisions based on your age, health, number of years before retirement, and the amount you have to invest.

- **Diversify globally.** Don't let national boundaries stand in your way. At the time of this writing, the U.S. dollar had depreciated against a broad range of currencies. Once you get comfortable with investing on your home turf, you might want to look for ways to capitalize on higher interest rates available in overseas markets, which include China, Brazil, Saudi Arabia, Canada, and various African countries.

- **Review your goals.** Read your responses in chapter 2 and use them as your guidelines when you plan investment strategies. This will keep you from letting fear or greed factor into your decisions.

- **Encourage younger family members to use the gift of time.** The website www.1stock1.com points out that if an eighteen-year-old invested $2,000 a year for ten years and never invested another cent, by the time that individual turned sixty-five, assuming a 9 percent rate of return, the magic of compounding will have turned that $20,000 into $800,000. Meanwhile, if that individual waited until the age of thirty-five to start investing $2,000 a year for thirty years, at the same 9 percent rate of return, that $60,000 investment will have compounded to $297,150 at the age of sixty-five. That's still an excellent return, but less than what can be earned over a longer period.

No matter your age, if you are a novice, try learning about investing by starting an investment club with family, friends, or a religious group. For free and helpful information on getting started, contact the nonprofit National Association of Investors Corporation (NAIC) online at www.betterinvesting.org or toll free at (877) 275-6242.

Members of the East End Baptist Church in Suffolk, Virginia, contacted the NAIC under the direction of the Reverend Dr. Mark A. Croston, Sr. This senior pastor initiated a novice investors club in 1996, asking members to contribute $25 a month as an instructional activity. This marked the first time that several of East End's older congregants had invested in the market. When the value of the group's portfolio went down during 2000 to 2002, Rev. Croston used the experience as a learning opportunity. "People were worried about losing their money, but I asked them what they would do if they went to a store and discovered that it was having a fifty-percent-off sale. They realized that when the market goes down, they need to know what to buy, because a downturn in the market is like going to a big sale."

Most of the members held fast, rode out the hard times, and watched their investments gain in value. More important, several have started investing on their own, in preparation for retirement. Rev. Croston believes investing changes the way an individual relates to the world. He tells of a parishioner who used to get annoyed when she had to stop her car at a railroad crossing as the Norfolk Southern train went by. But not anymore. She told Rev. Croston, "Now that I'm invested in the company, when those railroad cars go by, I'm thinking, *ca-ching, ca-ching*, like a cash register."

I'm glad that Rev. Croston brought up the fear people experience during market downturns, because that's a subject that often arises in my conversations with clients. I want to tell you about one of my clients, Ron Montgomery, and his approach to investments. This thirty-nine-year-old Virginia Beach doorman is on his way to making his second million, preparing for retirement at the age of fifty, by buying, remodeling, and selling moderately priced houses. He had, however, been reluctant to ride out the stock market when it was low.

Mr. Montgomery phoned me in 2008, during an economic

downturn marked by record home foreclosures and high oil prices, and said he'd purchased another rental unit. I asked why he was buying real estate when housing values were deflated, and he seemed shocked by my question. "Of course I'm buying. This is the time to get good deals. The housing market will come back, and when it does, those properties I purchased at a lower price will be worth a lot more, so I'll be worth a lot more, too."

"That's interesting," I said, "but that's also true about the stock market. So how come you won't do the same thing when it comes to investing in stocks and bonds?" He remained silent for a few minutes. Whenever the market went down, Mr. Montgomery phoned and insisted on moving his stock investments to something far more conservative or, more typically, to cash accounts. In this manner, he'd preserved his bottom line but missed out on opportunities to continue investing in stocks when the prices were good.

Think of some of the blue-chip offerings—let's picture Google and Wal-Mart, for example—and how Mr. Montgomery might have invested in companies that he might not otherwise have been able to afford. You can understand, then, why savvy investors like Rev. Croston and his East End club members have learned to ride out the hard times and wait for the economy to revive.

When you have a long-term horizon, at least five years before your retirement date, you have the time to buy low and sell high. An experienced investor knows that it's not the minute-to-minute value of a portfolio but the number of shares of quality stocks that really counts.

The East End Baptist investors can also serve as reminders of how important it is to make investing a consistent process in your life. It's as important as eating a healthy diet and exercising regularly. Once you incorporate investing into your life, you'll feel you're headed in the right direction.

When you're watching or listening to investment shows, jot down financial terms and phrases that are beginning to sound familiar and start using them in your conversations.

_____

_____

_____

BUILDING FINANCIAL LITERACY

The terms *bull market* and *bear market* are used to describe prolonged periods of market activity. Picture a sleepy bear hibernating in a cave and you can see why this motionless animal symbolizes a bear market, when stock prices fall in general. Bear markets typically occur during economic recessions, high unemployment, and rising inflation. In contrast, an aggressive, kicking bull symbolizes a time of upward stock market movement. Bull markets often occur during economic booms or recoveries, or when investors believe that the economy is moving on the right track.

CONSIDERING SCRIPTURE

"Then the one who had received the one talent also came forward, saying, 'Master, I knew that you were a harsh man, reaping where you did not sow, and gathering where you did not scatter seed; so I was afraid, and I went and hid your talent in the ground. Here you have what is yours.' But his master replied, You wicked and lazy slave! You knew, did you, that I reap where I did not sow, and gather where I did not scatter? Then you ought to have invested my money with the bankers, and on my return I would have received what was my own with interest. So take the talent from him, and give it to the one with the ten talents. For to all those who have, more will be given, and they will have an abundance; but from those who have nothing, even what they have will be taken away.' "   —Matthew 25:24–29.

If the spirit moves you, read this passage aloud and write about its meaning as you become more financially literate.

_____

_____

_____

_____

_____

_____

_____

STEP 8

Protect Your Assets

16

Selecting Insurance That Fits Your Needs

When I was a kid I sensed that there was something suspect about insurance agents dropping by homes in my neighborhood to pick up envelopes containing a dollar or less to pay for burial insurance, small policies that covered funeral services. I wasn't suspicious solely because most agents were white men who seemed to go out of their way for minimal sums, traveling through neighborhoods they might otherwise have avoided—because some of those agents were black. The practice just didn't feel right to me.

I realize now that these insurance agents recognized something essential about African Americans. Times were so hard for our ancestors that they could exert little control over their own lives. The agents sensed that burial insurance allowed black people at least to govern their last rites. Before insurance policies were available, slaves banded together and formed burial associations so they could help send one another to their "homecomings in glory." Commercial interests exploited our need for a secure end.

By the new millennium evidence suggested that insurance companies had cheated black consumers. Between 2000 and 2004, sixteen cases were settled in which it was found that black people had been charged as much as 33 percent more than whites for burial coverage. Insurance companies were required to repay more than $556 million, mostly in restitution to policyholders or their heirs. In many cases, those companies' agents had stopped by homes to keep an eye out for new members of each family, looking for opportunities to sell more policies rather than consolidate several of them into a single, more affordable one.

You might be thinking that the insurance industry, with its $25 trillion reserve, built partially on profits from nineteenth- and early-twentieth-century burial policies, should not be trusted, especially by black people. But as Great-Aunt Wa Wa used to say, "Don't throw out the baby with the bathwater." She meant, don't deprive yourself of the good to get rid of the bad.

Our forebears wisely paid to control that which they considered of paramount importance. Now it's up to us to keep moving forward, making sure that one single devastating event doesn't wipe out the wealth we have built. Today, though, we can do things differently. Before we sign insurance policies, we can develop a depth of understanding that can make us masters of our financial lives. This chapter offers the information you need for considering various types of insurance coverage. It is only a start. Be sure to ask a qualified financial consultant for advice on buying policies that meet your needs.

Remember that insurance is about risk management. If you're thinking of skipping this step, consider how you or your loved ones could survive without you as their main income source or if faced with mounting medical bills. Few people risk *not* insuring cars or homes, and they are compelled to purchase insurance by local laws and lending institutions. I'll focus on areas people tend to ignore at their own peril: life, health, and long-term-care insurance.

LIFE INSURANCE

The main types of life insurance offered are term and permanent. You can determine whether you need one or the other by considering your financial goals and how much time you need to reach them. Lisa and Montel Davis wrote at the top of their list of goals: "Educate our girls." When I began working with the couple in 1998, their daughters were ten and twelve. Mrs. Davis, forty-three, was a part-time clerk, and her husband, fifty-two, worked as a long-haul truck driver. After taxes, they brought home $37,000 annually in salaries, and paid $180 a month on a $50,000 permanent life insurance policy for Mr. Davis. "That fifty thousand dollars is enough to get the girls through college," Mrs. Davis explained.

It made sense that they'd chosen to insure Mr. Davis, since he provided most of the family's income. This is an easy call for singles, but if you are married and forced to decide which partner should be covered, I recommend choosing the major breadwinner.

Mr. and Mrs. Davis's $50,000 policy was *permanent life insurance*, which means that as long as the payments are made, the policy doesn't expire and is payable upon the holder's death. Permanent insurance is sometimes referred to as whole insurance, because it is designed to remain with you for the whole nine yards—all the way to the end. With permanent life insurance, your payments (called premiums) remain at a fixed rate. Generally speaking, the longer the policy remains in force, the greater the cash value. Once sufficient funds are contributed, you might be allowed to borrow or withdraw money against the policy. And if you stop making payments and surrender the policy, you might be entitled to receive a cash value.

When it comes to insurance needs, the most significant question is what's best for the consumer. A permanent life insurance policy was wrong for Mr. and Mrs. Davis. At $180 a month, they were not getting their money's worth of insurance. I often work with new clients who have been sold policies that don't fit their needs or their goals, and this was one of those cases.

The couple needed insurance that would cover them for fifteen years, after which their daughters would be finished with college and Mr. Davis would turn sixty-five, when he planned to retire. They needed but had not identified as a goal purchasing insurance that would protect their income. This is especially important when there are children or a spouse involved.

There's no hard science to figure out the right formula for how much insurance you need, but if you are the head of a household, multiply your annual salary by 10. For Mr. and Mrs. Davis, the permanent policy was insufficient because if he died, his wife would get $50,000, little more than a year's income—a figure that was woefully inadequate for maintaining the family's lifestyle. The couple needed more insurance, but $180 a month was their limit. When affordability is an issue, I often recommend purchasing term insurance.

Term life insurance covers an individual for a specified period, from one to thirty years. The advantage of term insurance rests in its affordability. Although term insurance premiums are not fixed and can increase, they remain relatively inexpensive and the policies are easy to understand—if you die after the term is expired, your beneficiaries get nothing. With Mr. and Mrs. Davis's permission, I requested quotes from several insurance companies. Based on Mr. Davis's age, gender, and good health, he was offered a fifteen-year term policy of $350,000 at the cost of approximately $180 a month, and he decided to take it.

Unfortunately, five years later Mr. Davis was killed in a truck collision. As you would expect, his family was devastated. Mrs.

Davis received the $350,000 in tax-free insurance money, but she didn't spend the money. At times like these, people often pay off mortgages and car notes and give something to their children. I advised Mrs. Davis that this could be a mistake with her retirement approaching. I suggested that she deposit her money in interest-bearing accounts and draw down 3 percent annually, a total of $10,500 a year or $875 a month. This was less than the interest she was earning. That, in addition to $2,200 she began receiving monthly as her husband's Social Security death benefit, would help her maintain the family's income.

After acting on that advice, she was able to stop working. A few years later her daughters entered college on scholarships, leaving their mother's savings intact. Five years later, Mrs. Davis has resisted dipping into the principal. She plans to leave it to her daughters.

I've included additional points that may help you determine—should you decide to purchase life insurance—whether your needs will best be met by term or permanent.

Advantages of Permanent Life Insurance

1. It allows you to leave a planned estate for beneficiaries.

2. It allows beneficiaries to pay off death taxes that will come due after the insured passes.

3. It allows for a mortgage to be paid off, so your property can be passed on to a loved one.

4. It allows you to leave a gift to your church or a charity.

5. It allows a spouse to pay off loans.

Advantages of Term Life Insurance

1. It is more affordable than permanent life insurance.

2. It is tailored for short-term needs, such as paying off a mortgage or educating children.

3. It gives peace of mind to those with a limited income.

4. It makes it easier to protect your income, allowing you to target, for instance, ten years of income in the death benefit. For example, if you earn $35,000 annually and have $100,000 saved, you could take out a $250,000 policy.

Burial Insurance

Burial policies are a form of permanent life insurance, since they are paid off when the individual dies. Some carriers continue to sell burial policies for a few dollars a week, sending out door-to-door agents or handling collections through automatic payroll deductions.

Because burial insurance can go into effect immediately, without blood and urine testing, some of my clients have chosen it when health conditions caused them to be denied more extensive coverage. If you are facing a similar challenge, try applying to several different companies for conventional coverage. Even when offered at competitive rates, burial policies are costlier than some other types of policies in the long run. If you have taken out more than one burial policy to cover other relatives, you might be able to save by having the policies consolidated.

Although medical exams are not usually required for burial insurance, consumers may be asked to swear that they don't reside in a nursing home and do not have HIV or AIDS. Other burial policies are available for people with serious health problems or terminal illnesses. It's important to be truthful in reporting on your health. As with all insurance policies, claims can be denied if there is proof of fraud.

HEALTH INSURANCE

Evidence suggests that not having health insurance can seriously harm your health. A Harvard University study found that people without coverage were found to suffer significantly worse outcomes with cardiovascular disease, diabetes, and cancer than those who had health insurance. Age can make a difference. According to the Harvard researchers, the uninsured "near elderly," those too young to qualify for Medicare—the federally funded medical insurance program for those sixty-five and older—got sick faster than comparable people with insurance.

Rising health-care costs help explain why I often meet people who are working to build wealth and yet haven't visited a doctor in more than a year. A Commonwealth Fund survey found that 33 percent of African Americans had no health coverage in 2005. In the past, many of us relied on employers for insurance. But with health-care costs rising at more than twice the rate of inflation, many businesses have stopped offering these benefits or have switched to part-time personnel so they won't have to offer them.

Not having health insurance can derail your retirement plans, and so can inadequate coverage. Hundreds of thousands of people are bankrupted each year by medical debts, and shockingly, two thirds of those surveyed in the Commonwealth study and three quarters of those in the Harvard study had health insurance.

If you don't have health insurance, do what you can to secure it, and when you do, get familiar with the terms of the coverage so you'll know how to prevent paying high out-of-pocket fees for using out-of-network providers. If you can't pay medical bills in full, avoid paying for them with credit cards when possible, which only drive up costs with high interest rates. According to a study by Access Project, a consumer advocacy group, and Demos, a public-policy research organization, 20 percent of households surveyed in 2005 had average credit card balances nearly $3,700 higher because of medical debt.

The message here is that health insurance is absolutely necessary for the sake of your health and your financial future. A single hospital stay can cost tens of thousands of dollars, and an accident or stroke requiring rehabilitation can saddle you with bills that will take years to repay. By delaying medical care you may become so unhealthy that you won't be able to qualify for insurance. Providing health insurance for yourself can be expensive, but it won't cost nearly as much as you might wind up paying without it. Here are some suggestions for getting health insurance.

- **Search for competitive rates.** Fill out an online application at www.ehealthinsurance.com. It's a good idea to take the quotes to an insurance professional, who might make a better offer or explain some of the more inscrutable terminology.

- **Find out what your state government offers.** Many states maintain websites listing reasonably priced health plans for individuals, small businesses, and the self-employed. Google your state along with "government" and "health insurance" for information.

- **Do a background check.** Before you choose a carrier, go online to the National Association of Insurance Commissioners at www.naic.org, and under the "Consumer Information Source" link, research companies that you're considering. If you find lots of complaints, delete those companies from your list.

- **Consider high deductibles for affordability.** If your priority is coverage in the event of a catastrophe, paying more out of pocket before you're reimbursed may not seem unreasonable. High-deductible, high-co-pay policies are preferable to no coverage, at least these policies cover the big medical bills.

- **Consider temporary health insurance.** Short-term policies fill in gaps between jobs so you can continue using your own doctors. Coverage is available from thirty days to a year and is usually cheaper than traditional health insurance. Begin your online search at www .assuranthealth.com.

- **Use your membership connections.** Contact trade, professional, union, alumni, fraternal, or community organizations to find out whether they offer affordable group health-insurance plans.

- **Utilize the law protecting laid-off employees.** COBRA (Consolidated Omnibus Budget Reconciliation Act) laws allow you to keep employee health-care insurance for eighteen months after your benefits end. The rates tend to be high, however.

- **Don't join the ranks of uninsured "too young" retirees.** If you're retiring before you qualify for Medicare, factor in costs for individual health insurance. Or ask your employer to let you continue paying for the company-sponsored health insurance. This can be helpful if you have a preexisting medical condition that makes it difficult to get individual coverage.

- **Before retiring, make sure you qualify for individual insurance.** If you don't qualify for Medicare and have an existing medical condition, such as high blood pressure, that might disqualify you in the individual market, shop around for coverage. If necessary, keep working until you find it.

- **Get clear on your employer-provided health benefits.** If you're sixty-five or older and planning on employer-sponsored health care as a primary source of coverage or as a Medicare supplement, find out whether your company plans to eliminate this benefit for you. And negotiate for health care in your retirement package.

- **Make sure you can take your insurance with you.** Some insurance carriers provide only a short list of contracted out-of-state medical providers. If you're moving to a new state, look carefully at your insurer's offerings in your new locale. You'll want to avoid paying a fortune in out-of-network claims.

- **Fight claim denials by insurers.** If you're stuck with a major bill, don't withdraw funds from your retirement account. Consider hiring a medical-claims professional to advocate for you. To contact the Alliance of Claims Assistance Professionals (ACAP), go online to www.claims .org.

- **Build a health savings account (HSA).** The amount of your deductible up to a certain cap determines how much you can contribute to an HSA each year. Once accumulated, your money can be withdrawn without tax penalty, as long as it's used for medical, vision, or dental care. Unspent money in these interest-earning accounts rolls over from one year to the next. Before you dip into these accounts, remember the magic of compounding and leave the money untouched until you're older. If your company doesn't offer HSAs, ask a human resources administrator to get the ball rolling, or contact an insurance agent. Familiarize yourself with the ground rules, and make sure that your health-insurance company qualifies. For more information, go online to www.hsainsider.com or www.hsadecisions .org.

LONG-TERM-CARE INSURANCE

Long-term-care insurance is a private policy designed to help pay for future nursing-home bills. The benefits are negligible and even nonexistent for low-income people with few assets who would qualify for Medicaid.

Along with annuities, long-term-care insurance draws some of the greatest number of consumer complaints, and that doesn't surprise me. I have met many people who have been duped into signing policies that they don't understand for extensive coverage that they don't need. People should buy long-term care policies for one of three reasons: (1) to give themselves peace of mind about whether there will be someone to care for them at their most advanced age; (2) to protect their assets; and (3) to preserve their estates. Let's examine these reasons more closely.

1. Peace of mind. People are living longer, and for many, their greatest fear is spending their last days with strangers in unfamiliar surroundings or becoming a burden to their family. Long-term-care insurance can help pay for nursing-home stays and cover home health care and adult day care (often used for those with dementia or Alzheimer's disease).

2. Asset protection. If you require nursing-home care, Medicare will only pay the costs after forcing your assets into liquidation and spending down your money to a few thousand dollars. Long-term-care insurance isn't a perfect solution. It usually doesn't foot the entire bill. If a nursing-home stay costs $160 a day, the policy might provide for $100, which leaves you with a $60-a-day charge. Individuals typically require about ninety days in a nursing-home facility, but should you need care for a longer period, the difference between what you would have to pay out of pocket versus what you would pay with insurance assistance could make the difference between whether or not you have a house to return to when you're released.

3. Estate preservation. An estate plan is simply a guide to how you want your affairs put in order after your death. It allows you to communicate to others how you want your possessions, property, and even debts discharged. Whatever your plans, you don't want to see them disrupted by the need for end-of-life uninsured long-term care of three to four years. Again, long-term-care insurance can allow your executors to keep your estate in place.

I've included five questions that I am often asked concerning this coverage:

1. When should I get long-term-care insurance?

You have to assess your situation to figure out the best age for buying this coverage. You don't want to wait too long. Consider this: If a forty-year-old man sustains major injuries in a car accident and is confined to a nursing home for two years, he might be able to return to work when he's forty-two and recover his assets. If a sixty-eight-year-old sustains those same injuries, it's unlikely he could return to work at seventy and recover financially if he didn't have long-term-care coverage.

You don't want to put off your decision so long that you wish you had been more proactive. And it's a lot cheaper to purchase LTC insurance at forty than when you're older. But at the same time, chances are you can wait until fifty if you don't take major physical risks, you're in good health, and you don't have a family history of chronic diseases (most insurers will reject you if you're ill). According to one school of thought, the best age range for purchasing LTC is sixty to sixty-five, since this is a period when individuals are more likely to have assets to protect and more money available for their own needs. Policy prices tend to get extremely high for those who wait until after sixty. I have clients seventy and older take out the coverage, even though their premiums are pricey, because they're willing to pay for peace of mind.

2. Wouldn't inflation affect the amount of coverage I'd be buying?

Absolutely. Your policy might pay $150 a day for nursing-home costs today. But let's say you don't need that care for another twenty years. That $150 wouldn't go far in 2029. That's why it's important to buy a policy with a cost-of-living adjustment (COLA) so you can keep pace with inflation. As the cost of living increases, so do benefits. It's equally important for you to analyze nursing-home costs in the state where you plan to retire, since prices vary considerably.

3. How can I make sure that an insurance company is reliable?

You can research the financial strength of a company and find out whether it has earned a reputation for reliability by looking at its credit ratings. Go online to www.standardandpoors.com. It's also important, once your contract arrives in the mail, to sit down with the agent who sold it to you, so you can make sure all the benefits you discussed have been included in that policy. Some people record their interviews with agents and review them later so they can recall the features they've discussed.

4. How can I get the most long-term-care coverage for my money?

There are two ways to save. The first is by limiting the duration of coverage. Most people don't need LTC insurance for their entire remaining life span but for periods when they are more likely to be confined to a nursing home. Lifetime LTC policies are prohibitively expensive and often unnecessary. If cost is a factor, purchase a policy that pays anywhere from four to eight years of benefits and that is triggered after you are certified as needing the care. Most people don't need more than that. In a study of more than 500,000 LTC policies that provided benefits of up to six years, it was found that only 5 percent of the policies were paid out for that long.

Another way to save is by extending the waiting period in your policy. A waiting period refers to the number of days before the insurer starts paying you benefits. Let's say you went into a nursing home and were willing to pay out of pocket for the first four months of your illness. The rule of thumb is, the longer the waiting period, the cheaper the policy, so it makes sense to extend the waiting period if you can afford it. Some policies offer discounts for couples, including unmarried partners.

Companies are increasingly offering group rates to employees for LTC. Although this might be less expensive than what you can buy on the commercial market, before you sign, make certain that your premium won't go up when you retire.

5. Do I need LTC insurance if I'm on Medicaid?

If you receive Medicaid, the government-funded medical assistance for people with low incomes, or Supplemental Security Insurance, the federally funded disability program, you probably don't need long-term-care coverage. After most of your financial resources have been depleted, Medicaid will pay for your long-term care. In fact, many people buy LTC insurance to avoid having their assets liquidated to clear the way for Medicaid coverage.

I hope I have convinced you of the importance of covering your life and assets. No one likes paying for coverage, but think of it as a self-esteem issue. If you work hard to build wealth, you deserve to have protection. Insurance is designed to keep money flowing. In chapter 18, you will learn how to pass gifts on to the next generation.

HELPFUL HINT

Powerful industries have lobbyists to represent their interests, and people fifty and over also have a highly effective advocacy group: AARP, formerly known as the American Association of Retired People. As the name change implies, you shouldn't wait until you're retired to join this nonprofit, nonpartisan organization. In addition to keeping politicians on issues concerning the over-fifty set, AARP offers access to health, auto, and home owners' insurance, and provides members with award-winning publications chock-full of financial-planning, consumer, and health information geared toward people who want to guard their most valuable treasure: their future. For more information, go online to www.aarp.org or phone (888) OUR-AARP.

BUILDING FINANCIAL LITERACY

When you want to add or change terms or conditions on an insurance contract, you're asking for a written form known as a rider. Policyholders have to pay extra for riders that provide enhancements, such as additional coverage for a spouse or child. Another example of a rider is a double indemnity, which gives beneficiaries twice the amount of the policy if the insured dies accidentally.

CONSIDERING SCRIPTURE

"Peace I leave with you; my peace I give to you. I do not give to you as the world gives. Do not let your hearts be troubled, and do not let them be afraid."

—John 14:27.

If the spirit moves you, read this passage aloud and write about its meaning as you become more financially literate.

_____

_____

_____

_____

_____

17

Keeping Income Flowing
for the Rest of Your Life

Frank Graham, sixty-seven, a former army officer, had retained his military bearing. He sat ramrod straight in my office, his wingtip shoes shined to a high gloss, as he spoke in a commanding baritone.

"Well, Smith, looks like I've actually put away enough to retire comfortably."

He sounded almost surprised that he had managed to reach this point.

After an army career, Mr. Graham worked as a Detroit auto executive, but in the early nineties his life unraveled. He would be the first to admit that his drinking and other aspects of his life destroyed his marriage and his career. In 1995 he was on the run from thugs who were pursuing him for gambling debts when he showed up in Norfolk, Virginia, at the door of his father's run-down one-bedroom home. The trunk of Mr. Graham's Lexus was filled with designer suits and shoes. His $300,000 retirement fund had been emptied. And his adult son and daughter were refusing to have anything to do with him.

Mr. Graham's father agreed to let him sleep on the sofa under two conditions: that he attend church three times a week and that he start working with me to plan for his future.

In our first meeting, Frank Graham was blasé while discussing a dismal credit report and credit card and loan debts totaling $110,000. When the subject turned to values, I asked him what mattered most to him. While he didn't betray his military reserve, his words signaled a depth of feeling. "I want my children back in my life, and for my father to be able to look me straight in the eye. He's ashamed of me."

The next Sunday morning, when the pastor at his father's church issued an altar call, Mr. Graham said he stood but couldn't find the strength to walk up front and commit to a new life. Someone came to his rescue. "A strong hand gripped my elbow, and I turned around. It was my father, and I saw hope in his eyes. He still believed in me. I started walking up that aisle, and six other men followed. I believe the Lord was telling me that I'm a leader. But what he was also saying was that I had to get out of the way first and allow him to take the lead."

From that point, Mr. Graham never wavered, despite several humiliating experiences. I had advised him to sell his luxury car, which he did, and he began driving his dad's clunker. With $12,000 from the sale of the car, he paid $2,000 each to his ex-wife and his church, $2,000 on debts, and $1,000 in rent to his father. With the balance, he started a retirement fund. After being turned down from one job after another, he was hired as a waiter for a restaurant chain.

At the end of each shift, he refused to exchange the quarters and crumpled dollars he'd received in tips into larger bills, because, he said, counting out the coins and bills gave him a newfound respect for money. Sunday mornings he divided his tips into glass jars and split his proceeds between the church, his ex-wife, his father, and his savings account. He used his salary for living expenses and to pay down his loans and credit card debts. As his financial literacy increased and he saw how his balances were growing from compounded interest, he started working a double shift to pay down his bills faster.

Three years into his new life, his father died, leaving Mr. Graham the tiny house they'd shared. It was too run-down to sell, so he came up with a better idea. He took classes and learned how to remodel it himself, adding a guest room. He was also promoted to assistant manager, and he reunited with his adult children. In fact, one of the reasons he was so determined to retire was to spend more time with his grandchildren.

"So, where do we go from here, Smith?" Mr. Graham asked.

Maybe you're asking the same question about yourself. Throughout this work, you've learned that the world is awash in money, and I've outlined strategies to help you make more of that money flow in your direction. This chapter is written to help you set up an income stream that can last the rest of your life.

You can record any financial changes that have occurred since you began working on this book. Don't feel discouraged if you haven't made any major changes yet. Remember that when I discuss clients, I condense the details of their progress. It doesn't happen for anyone overnight. What's most important is whether your knowledge has increased and whether you have a better sense about what you have to do.

If you have used the tracking forms at the back of the book, it will be easy to fill in this data. If you have been working through the steps, you may enjoy the immediacy of updating your expenses in this chapter. Be sure to compare the itemized areas and totals to help hone in on expenditures that you might want to adjust. If you haven't made any changes and need to, you can revisit this section at that time, but for now skip to "Your Net Worth."

UPDATED PERSONAL AND FAMILY MONTHLY EXPENSES

Category	Current-Updated Amount
Books/periodicals	
Care for parents or other extended family	
Child care/after-school programs	
Child's allowance Child support	
Church donations (tithe)	
Dental	
Eating out	
Education for children (tuition, tutors, books, school supplies, field trips, etc.)	
Education/yours	
Education/spouse	

Category	Current-Updated Amount
Groceries	
Hair care/yours Hair care/spouse Hair care/child's	
Health care: insurance, copays, prescriptions	
Household staples: cleaning products, lightbulbs, etc.	
Laundry/dry cleaning	
Manicure/pedicure	
Pet care	
Phones: Cell Home	
Public transportation	
Self-improvement	
Vacations	
Miscellaneous	
Unexpected	
Total	$

After totaling your monthly expenses, please add them up for the monthly total and then figure out your additional monthly costs:

EXPENSES FOR HOME/ OTHER PROPERTY

Category	Current-Updated Amount
Mortgage	
Home-equity loan	
Real estate tax	
Rent payment	
Home owner's insurance	
Home owner fees	
Electricity	
Gas/oil	
Trash pickup	
Water	
Sewer	
Cable or satellite TV	
Internet	

Category	Current-Updated Amount
Unexpected	
Yard and garden care	
Major repair	
Regular repair	
Furniture	
Household help	
Additional real estate	
Other	
Total	$

CAR EXPENSES

Category	Current-Updated Amount
Car loan/lease payment Second-car loan	
Insurance	
Fuel	

(continued)

Category	Current-Updated Amount
Fuel for spouse	
Repairs/maintenance	
Parking, tolls	
Car wash	
Total	$

BUSINESS EXPENSES

Category	Current-Updated Amount
Bank fees	
Club dues	
Credit card debt	
Office supplies	
Loans	
Miscellaneous	
Post office	

Category	Current-Updated Amount
Student loans	
Unreimbursed business	
Total	$

TAXES

Category	Current-Updated Amount
Your FICA	
Spouse's FICA	
Your Medicare	
Spouse's Medicare	
Your federal income	
Spouse's federal income	
Your state income	
Spouse's state income	
Total	$

MONTHLY CONTRIBUTIONS
TOWARD INVESTMENTS

Category	Increase or Decrease Planned
Stocks/bonds/mutual funds	
Your life insurance	
Spouse's life insurance	
Other insurance	
401(k)-type retirement fund	
Other financial plans or invest-ments to which you contribute	
Total	$

TOTAL EXPENDITURES

Personal/family	$
Home/other property	$
Car	$
Business	$
Investments	$
Grand total	$

INCOME

Yours	
Spouse's	
Alimony/child support	
Real estate	
Business	
Total	$

Finally, subtract what you spend from the amount you have coming in.

Incoming $_____
Outgoing (minus) –$ _____
Cash flow $_____

YOUR NET WORTH

It will be interesting to note any changes in your cash flow. Now it's time to work on your net worth statement, which is a snapshot of your financial assets and liabilities. Here's what Mr. Graham's looked like:

FRANK GRAHAM: STATEMENT OF NET WORTH, OCTOBER 2007

Assets		Liabilities	
Cash	$ 108,000	Home-improvement loan	$ 39,000
Qualified investments	$ 71,000	Daughter's student loan	$ 6,000
Nonqualified investments	$ 69,000		
Home	$ 114,000		
Other assets	$		
Car	$ 21,000		
Motor home	$ 27,000		
Total assets	$ 410,000	**Total liabilities**	$ 45,000
		Net worth	**$ 365,000**

A decade of hard work and playing catch-up—utilizing tax provisions that allow people over fifty to increase tax-deferred savings—allowed Mr. Graham to build a comfortable nest egg. He started out with a net worth of negative $98,000, but his nest egg grew along with his financial literacy. Now you can create your own statement.

__(your name)__: STATEMENT OF NET WORTH, ____(date)____

Assets		Liabilities	
Cash			
Investments			
Home			
Other assets			
Total assets	$	**Total liabilities**	$
		Net worth	$

As you've probably guessed, Mr. Graham still had more planning ahead of him. His next step was to project how much he would need to live comfortably in retirement. He recorded a mortality date of one hundred. He was clearly feeling optimistic about his future. With an estimated thirty-three years in retirement, at $4,000 a month—at inflation-adjusted figures, and $48,000 annually—he would need $1,584,000.

Upon hearing figures like this, many clients groan—but not those who understand the process.

Mr. Graham's estimated Social Security income of $1,760 a month for thirty-three years would total $696,960.

His $1,200-a-month military pension for thirty-three years would total $475,200.

He purchased a commercial annuity that would pay $848 a month, which, over thirty-three years, would total $335,808.

He planned to withdraw 3.5 percent annually from his savings, a total of $3,780 annually. By earning a minimum of 5–6 percent a year on his cash account, he would never have to touch the principal and could live off the interest, approximately $161,460.

He added up his income:

Social Security	$696,000
Pension	$475,200
Commercial annuity	$335,808
Cash	$108,000
Total	$1,615,008

His number, the amount he calculated he would need for his life-time, was $1,584,000. His retirement income would leave him with a surplus of about $31,008, more than enough, especially because he hadn't figured in how much more money he would save by working part-time for the restaurant chain, which he was planning to do for the foreseeable future.

When he left my office that day, I couldn't help but notice that he was a very different man from the one I'd met a decade earlier. Now he was holding his head high and his steps appeared lighter.

Here's how you can figure out how much you'll need during retirement.

If you're planning to move to a new location, get busy looking into your prospects. After you've done your research and honed in on a location, if you aren't familiar with the area, spend at least several weeks of vacation—even six months if possible—living there. You don't want to find yourself stuck in a place you don't like. And remember that people often say they enjoy being close to loved ones, especially as they age. Once you've found a place where you can be happy, you can estimate housing costs.

Also, keep in mind that once you retire, your spending will go down for the following reasons:

1. You'll no longer be saving for retirement.

2. You'll no longer be paying Medicare and Social Security.

3. Your taxes might be lower (the amount varies, depending on your situation and location; you might have to con-sult your tax specialist after you come up with final fig-ures).

4. Your mortgage might be paid off.

5. Your children will be on their own—and you might no longer be paying to help support a parent or other extended-family members.

6. You will no longer need to spend as much on clothing and dry cleaning.

7. Your transportation costs might go down.

But depending on your circumstances, you may be paying more for health care.

Now you can estimate your expenses during retirement.

ESTIMATED EXPENSES DURING RETIREMENT

Category	Monthly	Annually
Books/periodicals		
Church donations (tithe)		
Dental		
Eating out		
Education/yours		

Category	Monthly	Annually
Education/spouse		
Groceries		
Hair care/yours Hair care/spouse		
Health care: Insurance, copays, prescriptions		
Household staples—cleaning products, lightbulbs, etc.		
Laundry/dry cleaning		
Manicure/ pedicure		
Pet care		
Phones: Cell Home		
Public transportation		
Self-improvement		
Vacations		

(continued)

Category	Monthly	Annually
Miscellaneous		
Unexpected		
Total	$	$

After totaling your weekly expenses, please add them to calculate the monthly total and then add monthly costs:

EXPENSES FOR HOME/OTHER PROPERTY DURING RETIREMENT

Category	Monthly	Annually
Mortgage		
Home-equity loan		
Real estate tax		
Rent payment		
Home owner's insurance		
Home owner fees		
Electricity		

Category	Monthly	Annually
Gas/oil		
Trash pickup		
Water		
Sewer		
Cable or satellite TV		
Internet		
Unexpected costs		
Yard and garden care		
Major repair		
Regular repair		
Furniture		
Household help		
Additional real estate		
Other		
Total	$	$

CAR EXPENSES
DURING RETIREMENT

	Monthly	Annually
Car loan/lease payment Second-car loan		
Insurance		
Fuel Fuel for spouse		
Repairs/ maintenance		
Parking, tolls		
Car wash		
Total	$	$

BUSINESS EXPENSES
DURING RETIREMENT

Category	Monthly	Annually
Bank fees		
Club dues		

Category	Monthly	Annually
Credit card debt		
Office supplies		
Loans		
Miscellaneous		
Post office		
Student loans		
Unreimbursed business		
Total	$	$

TAXES DURING RETIREMENT

	Monthly	Annually
Your federal income		
Spouse's federal income		
Your state income		
Spouse's state income		
Total	$	$

MONTHLY CONTRIBUTIONS TOWARD INVESTMENTS DURING RETIREMENT

Category	Increase or Decrease Planned
Stocks/bonds/mutual funds	
Your life insurance	
Spouse's life insurance	
Other insurance	
Savings	
Total	$

TOTAL EXPENDITURES DURING RETIREMENT

Personal	$
Home/other property	$
Car	$
Business	$
Investments	$
Grand total	$

Now multiply this grand total by 12 and then by the number of years you expect to live in retirement.

$_____ per year × _____ (# of years) = $_____

ESTIMATED INCOME DURING YOUR YEARS IN RETIREMENT

	Monthly	Annual	× Years in Retirement
Social Security/ yours			
Social Security/ spouse			
Pension			
Savings			
Annuities			
Rental			
Investments			
Total			$

Now you can subtract what you need from the amount you have coming in.

Incoming $ _____

Outgoing (minus) –$ _____

Cash flow $ _____

Adjust for inflation using the table below; I've included directions, in case you've forgotten how to use it.

INFLATION-FACTOR TABLE

Number of years until retirement	5	10	15	20	25
Inflation factor: 3%	1.16	1.34	1.56	1.81	2.09
Inflation factor: 4%	1.22	1.48	1.80	2.19	2.67

You can adjust for inflation using 3 percent, which is the average historical rate. You'll notice that the table indicates changes in increments of five years. If you're retiring in less than five years or just over ten, choose the closest number. The inflation-factor numbers are mathematical formulas that help break down complex numbers. Inflation rates can change. It's always helpful to keep apprised of changing economic trends by using online sites such as www.inflationdata.com (go to "Inflation" and then "Current Inflation"). You can also find longer periods on this website.

My number, adjusted for inflation	$ _____
Minus amount needed during retirement	–$ _____
Difference	$ _____

If you're looking at a shortfall, you might want to consider postponing retirement and working a few extra years to increase your income. Give it a lot of thought. You wouldn't want to quit a high-paying job and then realize you should have stayed. But if you have a defined/traditional pension, it might be to your advantage to quit so you can start receiving your pension payments and then get a part-time job to supplement your income for retirement.

I have many clients who have learned to scale back quite a bit to make their retirement income stretch over their lifetimes. The key, as always, is planning. You might want to rethink your retirement estimates and make decisions on the basis of what you can afford to do. It might be necessary to trade down to a smaller house, for example, or move to a state with lower tax rates. If you need to live on less, start practicing now, so you can pull it off in retirement.

Here are some other tips for keeping your money flowing for a lifetime:

- **Beware of debt.** It can creep up on people as they enjoy their early years of retirement and the sense of freedom it can impart. Remember, if you have to charge it and pay interest, you can't afford it.

- **If you're retiring early.** Make maximum contributions, utilizing the so-called catch-up provisions that allow those fifty and older to contribute additional amounts to retirement accounts. While you can take advantage of tax rules that will give access to your 401(k)-type retirement savings, if possible, let that money continue to grow and compound, and live off money in unqualified accounts. Since you won't yet qualify for Medicare, and if you aren't going to continue with employer-sponsored medical coverage, consider the health-insurance information in chapter 16. You'll want to safeguard against having your plans derailed by unplanned medical bills.

- **Don't feel obligated to tailor your retirement to your spouse's.** A lot of people feel they have to retire at the same time their spouse does, but perhaps you need to spend a few extra years on the job to build up your retirement savings or boost your Social Security benefits. If one of you is retiring and you want to learn to spend less, try living on one salary and socking away the rest.

- **If divorcing, don't sign away retirement benefits.** Many divorcing spouses make the mistake of taking the house instead of a share of the pension and lifetime benefits. Work with a financial professional to see whether this would be in your best interest.

- **Use calculated draw-down amounts.** Seek professional advice about how much you can pay yourself each year while keeping your nest egg intact. For example, you might be able to keep the principal of your savings intact by withdrawing no more than 4 percent interest a year, then increasing the amount you're taking ($10,000 annually, for example) by 3 percent to cover the costs of inflation (so the following year, the amount would become $10,300). Adjust the withdrawal amount each year to keep pace with inflation.

- **Be mindful of the red zone.** This is the term Prudential Insurance uses to describe the five years before and five years after retirement, a critical decade, when your behaviors serve as a bellwether as to how well you will manage your investment resources. The first five years of the retirement red zone are generally considered a time when investment risks should be reduced because there is not much time to recover from financial losses. During this period, some people feel so euphoric when experiencing freedom from rigid schedules that they overspend. Savvy retirees learn to preserve their nest eggs to make them last a lifetime.

- **Continue to consult a financial professional.** After you retire, you'll want to make sure you're still on track with your plans and see whether your investments need to be rebalanced.

HELPFUL HINT

If you have a home that you want to safeguard for your church or loved ones, who might not be able to pay high inheritance taxes, call an attorney and ask about a qualified residence trust (QRT), which decreases taxes at the time the residence is inherited. You would live in the house for the number of years specified in the trust and have control over the house, but the title would be transferred to the QRT.

BUILDING FINANCIAL LITERACY

It seems as if there's always one more tax to pay. But the marital deduction suggests that Uncle Sam has a heart when it comes to leaving spouses property. If you're married and want to transfer assets to your spouse upon your death, the marital deduction, a provision of the Economic Recovery Tax Act, allows for an unlimited amount of property transference, and there's no estate or gift tax.

" 'For surely I know the plans I have for you,' says the Lord, 'plans for your welfare and not for harm, to give you a future with hope.' "   —Jeremiah 29:11.

If the spirit moves you, read this passage aloud and write about its meaning as you become more financially literate.

_____

_____

_____

_____

_____

_____

_____

_____

_____

18

Choosing a Financial Professional

Now that you've become more financially literate, you're ready to interview financial planners. There are plenty who are quite good. The trick is to find the right person to serve your needs and whom you can trust. Start your search by asking your lawyer, tax preparer, bank manager, friends, relatives, and co-workers for recommendations. Some people meet financial professionals when they attend workshops or seminars or get advice from a firm offered by an employer. *No matter how you learn of a candidate, research is essential.* A title isn't the most important aspect. You want to find an adviser who is not trying to push a financial product and one who is qualified to help you meet your financial goals, such as retirement planning or sending your kids to college. Perhaps your goals have shifted as you continued this work. Either way, it will help to list them:

Goals to Discuss with a Financial Planner

1. _____

2. _____

3. _____

4. _____

5. _____

Feel free to ask for suggestions from people in your community that you don't know personally. Look up a few successful individuals—perhaps you have contact with them through church, or your child or grandchild, but that's not even necessary. Don't be shy about asking for information. Financially successful people got that way through good advice, and they are usually glad to network in this manner. Here's a place for you to record the names and numbers that you collect.

Financial Planners and Phone Numbers

1. _____

2. _____

3. _____

4. _____

5. _____

Even if you don't plan to invest in the stock market, it's a good idea to find a financial planner who is personally registered as an investment adviser, so you can research this person's background through the Financial Industry Regulatory Authority (FINRA). This nonprofit organization gathers a wealth of data on security firms and stockbrokers, including employment and exam history, and discloses whether individuals have been sued or had consumer complaints lodged against them. You can phone FINRA's hot line at (800) 289-9999 or go online to www.FINRA.org. Explain that you are looking for a financial planner and that you want to interview this individual in person or on the phone. If the interview is conducted in person, you may want to tape the conversation so you can review it later. You will want to complete a checklist for each interview.

CHECKLIST

Name of Financial Planner

_____

Dates of conversations _____ _____ _____ _____

Appointment date and time _____ _____

Professional designation (adviser, investment
   broker, etc.) _____

Name of office contact _____

Name of company _____

Address _____

_____

Phone number _____

E-mail address _____

Here are some questions to ask:

1. What are your areas of specialization?

   _____

   _____

   _____

2. Do you have experience in retirement planning, investment planning, or insurance planning? (Circle responses and add any other areas of specialty.)

   _____

3. How many years have you been in business?

   _____

4. What designations or certifications do you hold?

   _____

   _____

   _____

5. What licenses do you hold?

   _____

   _____

   _____

6. Are you personally registered as an investment adviser with the state or federal government in any of those capacities? (If the answer is no, ask why not.) Is your firm registered?

_____

_____

_____

_____

_____

_____

7. Did you work with another adviser or group before this? (Write the address or name of place where this person worked before.)

_____

_____

8. Which of your experiences prepared you for work in your field of expertise?

_____

_____

9. What do you charge? What kind of agreement would I have to sign?

10. Would I work with you directly?

_____

_____

_____

11. Are you independently employed?

Yes _____

No _____ (If the answer is no, ask "Who do you work for?") Also ask: "What's your affiliation with the companies whose products you sell? Do you earn commissions from selling their financial products? How are you paid for your work?"

_____

_____

_____

_____

_____

_____

12. What's your method for working with clients? Where would we begin, and what would be expected of me? When I'm finished, what's the end product? Would I continue working with you in the future?

_____

_____

_____

If an adviser responds to your questions with impatience, this is not the person for you. It's your money, so act assertively. I'm always impressed by potential clients who grill me about my work. If I were interviewing a financial adviser, I would ask to see her personal investment portfolio as one way of showing her knowledge. So far, no one has ever asked to see mine. As you've probably noticed, I never mind when clients are skeptical, because we're talking about their hard-earned money.

After you've completed two or three interviews—more if necessary—and have found someone you're comfortable with, make an appointment to meet, and plan to arrive early. If other clients are waiting, you can start a conversation and ask questions about whether this client has worked with the adviser for long. If so, get feedback.

Once you decide on an adviser, remember that it's never advisable to write a check to this individual or this individual's firm for financial products. If you're buying a commercial annuity, for instance, the check should be written directly to the insurance company, with a contract number written on the memo line. And, of course, a legitimate financial adviser would never ask for personal access to your checking or savings account. If accounts are opened on your behalf, they should be in your name, and you should have control and access to them so you can check regularly on your balances.

Remember that while you seek a professional for advice, it's your job to manage your own money and to research the companies you're paying. You'll want to protect your assets for your future as well as for your loved ones.

HELPFUL HINT

Sign up for a financial-literacy workshop so you can continue to expand your knowledge about money. Community colleges and commercial learning centers often offer these. You can also ask your human resources director to arrange a seminar for employees. The Heartland Institute works with local financial educators to conduct workplace seminars. For more information on Heartland seminars, call toll-free: (888) 895-1479 or go to their website at www.heartland financialeducation.com.

BUILDING FINANCIAL LITERACY

It may be one of the best baby gifts available. Parents, grandparents, and other extended-family members can set up education savings accounts (ESAs) to help pay for a child's future education expenses at accredited elementary and secondary schools, colleges, and universities. In 2007, a maximum of $2,000 a year could be contributed in a child's name to an ESA. Although these deposits are not tax-deductible, the income in the ESA compounds tax-free. You can learn more about purchasing an ESA through a financial adviser.

"The good leave an inheritance to their children's children." —Proverbs 13:22.

If the spirit moves you, read this passage aloud and write about its meaning as you become more financially literate.

_____

_____

_____

_____

_____

_____

_____

_____

_____

_____

STEP 9

Enjoy the Richness
of Your Life

19

Leaving a Legacy

I can't count the number of clients who have told me that they wish they had started working with me before they squandered inheritances they received from their parents. They look at me as if expecting me to chime in and help them castigate themselves for wasting the money, homes, and land that their parents bequeathed them.

So they're surprised when I tell them that money isn't everything.

Let me back up long enough to say that building wealth and passing it on to enrich the lives of your children and your children's children *is* one of the most important steps we can take as African Americans. Now that you have progressed this far in your journey, you know how to create income streams by delaying retirement, boosting income, borrowing less, paying yourself more, and purchasing annuities and insurance that can help you leave a bequest for loved ones.

We've explored options for keeping ahead of inflation so you won't wind up scrambling at the end of your life. You've learned how to put a house in trust so that loved ones won't lose the equity that has been built up because they can't afford to pay the taxes. You've learned, too, that buying long-term-care insurance can prevent situations in which property is seized by the government to pay for nursing-home expenses. Perhaps you have taped a picture inside this cover of a relative or African American hero or heroine, a financial role model, such as Oseola McCarthy, the laundress who lived beneath her means and was therefore able to provide college educations for a new generation of black youth. All of that is a reminder that money is absolutely important. But I'll say it again: It is not everything.

There is something every bit as significant to pass along that can change the lives of future generations, and that is to teach your children, grandchildren, and nieces and nephews about financial literacy. When a child is born, instead of putting a lot of money into fancy new clothes that they will soon outgrow, open an educational savings account in his or her name. (ESAs were described at the end of the previous chapter, under "Building Financial Literacy.")

Teach your children some of the financial definitions included in the literacy building blocks placed throughout this book. Don't nag them about money, making the thought of saving onerous, but use your good instincts to figure out the best way to teach the art of living beneath one's means. One approach to raising children with healthy attitudes about money is to refrain from discussing your finances with them when you are angry, hurt, or resentful. In addition to serving as an example for living abundantly on less, here's how you can raise financially literate children.

RAISING FINANCIALLY LITERATE CHILDREN

Age five and older

1. Don't raise children with memories of unplanned shopping trips in which you spend with abandon. Encourage your child to help you make a grocery list and to abide by it once you arrive at the store. When he's a little older, play a math game together of adding up the prices of items that you didn't buy. Keep adding them up week after week, month after month, taping together one page after another until you have a roll of paper covered with items and amounts that add up to a fantastic sum. When you reach $1,000, tear up the list to explain how a lot of people throw away money, just like that.

2. Surprise your child by saying you've decided to enjoy some of the money you've saved for an outing to a zoo or movie or some other fun trip. Take a photo of that happy day together and post it on the refrigerator, explaining that it might not have been possible had you not saved some money.

3. Give your child three piggy banks (or Mason jars) and label them "Saving," "Spending," and "Sharing." Set up little chores that allow the child to earn three of the same coins: pennies, nickels, dimes, quarters, silver dollars, or two-dollar coins. This makes for easy division, so she can learn the importance of putting some money aside, having fun with some of it, and giving some of it back to the Lord, whether to the church or other charitable organizations to help less fortunate individuals.

4. When coins fill the savings jar, take them to the bank and host an opening-a-savings-account ceremony, introducing your child to a bank manager, and allowing her to drop the coins into a change counter before depositing the money. Offer to match a percentage of some of her continued savings.

5. Divide monetary birthday and Christmas gifts into the same trio of spending, saving, and sharing, rather than giving toys or electronic devices that will be broken and discarded.

6. Give your child an allowance. No matter how small the amount, this gives a child a chance to follow the spending, sharing, and saving theme and to learn to make decisions about money.

7. For gift amounts over five dollars, give a check so you can teach your child about checking and banking accounts.

8. Encourage small business enterprises, from bake sales to garage sales to lemonade stands, and encourage your child to use the three-way plan.

9. Wake up one morning and tell your child that some of the most important things in life can't be purchased, and that you want to spend the day just laughing and having fun together. Take a photo that day and post it on the refrigerator.

10. Watch cartoons or any children's show together, and when it's over, discuss the commercial messages and the pressures that companies put on viewers to buy their products—often items that aren't necessary.

Adolescents and teenagers (in addition to some of the previously mentioned activities)

1. Make bread or rolls together. As the dough rises, explain compound interest and how, like the dough, compounding is barely noticeable at first, and then the amount seems to expand magically. Explain how compound interest can work for you as a saver and against you as a borrower.

2. Give a share of stock from a company that's popular with young people. Explain what stocks are. Teach him to keep track of the stock's worth at the end of a year.

3. When the time is appropriate, help prepare postcards that can be mailed to friends and family announcing that your teenager is available for babysitting and other chores that will allow him to earn money for not only spending, sharing, and for paying himself—but also for investing.

4. Plan a vacation day for visiting a stock market in your area, and take a tour.

5. Subscribe to *Black Enterprise*, and read it together along with other books, so you can model the importance of reading— and of reading about enterprising and financially savvy African Americans.

6. As a birthday gift, announce that your teenager is old enough to research a company to invest in. Buy a share in the selected company.

7. Give your child two $50 bills. Sign your name on one bill and tell him that the unsigned bill is for sharing, spending,

and saving but that if he can hold onto the other bill for a year, he can have that, plus another $50 to spend, share, and save.

8. Set aside regular times for paying bills, and invite your teenager to make out the checks as you pay creditors and yourself.

9. Join with other parents and grandparents to help your teenager start a youth investment club.

SHARE THIS ADVICE WITH NEW COLLEGE GRADUATES

Don't let education loans get you down

As a result of skyrocketing tuition costs and changes in federal funding, you might be one of millions graduating with the highest student-loan balances in U.S. history. But don't despair. Your degree increases your chances of earning nearly double what you would earn without one. If you're still in school, talk to a financial-aid officer and make sure you understand the terms for repaying the loan. Paying on time might qualify you for the lowest interest rate. And it's easier to make due dates consistently if you have payments deducted automatically from your checking account or if you pay online. Also, keep in mind that some of your loan can be "forgiven" by the government if you're willing to work in economically depressed areas, teach at a public school, or volunteer for programs such as the Peace Corps, VISTA, or the AmeriCorps teaching program. For more information, go to http://studentaid.ed.gov and type in "forgiveness," or go to www.finaid.org/loans/forgiveness.phtml, or Google AmeriCorps.

Think of credit cards as dangerous necessities

Sure you will need at least one to establish a credit history, but don't use it until you have the money to pay it off immediately. Credit card debt is the downfall of many hardworking individuals. If you already owe a credit card company, you might want to pay that balance off before any other debt (and always on time, so you don't ruin your credit) because the high interest rate will compound and leave you with a bill that is higher than the original cost of the item. Also, start an emergency fund as soon as you're employed, so you can dip into it, rather than use a credit card, in times of crisis.

Get health insurance

One of the harshest facts of life is that once you graduate, your parents' insurers will boot you from your family's policy. If you're young and healthy, you might assume you can do without coverage of your own, but don't take the chance. One accident during a basketball game or tripping on subway stairs will leave you with medical bills that will burden you for years. Go online to e-insure.com or ehealthinsurance.com to search for low-cost insurance. If you think you can't afford health insurance of any kind and you haven't graduated, ask your parents or grandparents who might be planning to give you a graduation gift to instead foot the bill for a year or six months worth of your health insurance. Once you get coverage, be sure to read carefully the terms of your policy, and get a listing of the company's in-network physicians, laboratories, therapists, et cetera, so you don't wind up paying high out-of-pocket fees. For the same reason, check with the insurer first before going to a new medical facility.

For the first two years, phone from home and rent movies

If your parents aren't paying for a cell phone, consider doing without one for a while, and rent movies rather than signing up for cable

TV or spending a lot of money at the movies. The money you save during your twenties has greater financial power than what you invest after thirty, because of the long-term effects of compounding. Imagine that at the age of twenty-five, you invest $4,000 a year for ten years and then stop and never add another cent to the retirement account. The money is not withdrawn and continues to grow through the process of compounding, when gains are realized on the original investment, and then a greater return is realized on top of that, and so on, year after year. It's almost magical the way compounding works, yet it's a financial reality. When you're sixty, that $40,000 investment will have grown to $690,709.* Maybe at your age $4,000 a year sounds like a lot of money, but let me explain why I'm suggesting you sock it away now. If you instead wait until you're thirty-five to start putting away $4,000 a year and keep saving that amount yearly until you're sixty, you will have put in a total of $100,000, but your account will be worth only $315,818—less than half as much if you'd started ten years earlier. That's why, after you get a job, if you pretend for a few years that you don't have much more than you had in college and live beneath your means, you can plow money into tax-deferred vehicles and, I hope, retire rich.

If your employer offers matching 401(k)-type funds, accept them

You might want to reread chapter 5 to learn why 401(k)-type plans are so important. Not contributing to one of these funds is like throwing money away. And if you change jobs, don't cash out the money in your account, or you'll pay up-front penalties.

---

* Investment results may vary, and positive returns from investing in the stock market are never guaranteed.

Sharing your knowledge with someone who can pass it on to future generations is one form of passing on a legacy. The next and final chapter can help you find ways to take some of the skills you honed in your professional life and use them in a new way to give back to the community.

HELPFUL HINT

Write a description of the kind of work you'd like to do in a new life. For the time being, don't get caught up in how you can afford it, just take this time to dream. Describe your dream vocation.

———————————————————————————

———————————————————————————

———————————————————————————

———————————————————————————

Now ask yourself what you can do, given your newfound financial knowledge, to pursue those dreams. Don't dismiss the idea. Your growing financial literacy can make what appears to be impossible possible.

BUILDING FINANCIAL LITERACY

Most people realize that it makes sense to write a will—naming heirs, explaining what they'll receive, and appointing an executor—but they might not have considered establishing a trust, which is a legal document written with an eye toward the future. People usually associate trusts with the superwealthy, but they can also help those with estates worth $50,000 or more. For example, you want to retain access to your assets, but in looking toward the future, you want to ensure that someone pays your bills and makes certain you're given the best care, should you become disabled or cognitively impaired. In that case, you might set up a living trust and designate an alternate trustee. After your death, the trustee would distribute your assets to beneficiaries. Some trusts are designed to exert control over how assets are handed down to heirs. For instance, it might stipulate that the inheritance must be spent on a grandchild's tuition; given out as a reward for good grades; donated to your church to establish an after-school program; or withheld if someone isn't drug-free or sober. A trust can shield money from a divorcing son- or daughter-in-law. Estate-planning attorney Melanie Lee, of Richmond, Virginia, suggests talking openly about your goals with someone who specializes in estate planning.

CONSIDERING SCRIPTURE

"Do not neglect the gift that is in you, which was given to you through prophecy with the laying on of hands by the council of elders." —1 Timothy 4:14.

If the spirit moves you, read this passage aloud and write about its meaning as you become more financially literate.

_____

_____

_____

_____

20

Reinventing Your Life

You might not recognize it, but you've been given another gift. Maybe you've overlooked it and can only claim it now. You already know that, thanks to medical science, you have an opportunity to live longer than those of generations past. That can be bad news for someone lacking in financial literacy. But as you develop financial know-how, you can use these extra years to reinvent your life.

Folks are always talking about what they would do if they could go back and start all over again. You can do something better than starting over. You can take all the hard-won wisdom that's a result of your failures, losses, successes, and expertise, combine it with your financial know-how, and use it to go forward. I'm not promising it will be easy, but it can propel you into a new life.

Perhaps you're planning a future in which you move to a new area, start a business, search for part-time work, dedicate your time to charitable causes, or maybe begin an entirely new career. If you aren't weighed down by concerns about money, you will have a lighter load and therefore more energy than you've had in years. Medical science has given you opportunities to live longer. Reading this book might have increased your financial literacy. And God has given you hope and talent and energy.

I've told you about clients who turned their lives around with financial acumen. Now let me tell you about my coauthor, Brenda Lane Richardson. Before we started this book together, I suggested that she and her husband, Mark, an Episcopal priest, might first want to work through the retirement-planning process so she could understand it well enough to write about it.

Initially she was reluctant, more embarrassed than anything, that they'd delayed getting their financial lives together. This was early 2006; Brenda was fifty-eight and Mark, fifty-seven. They'd raised three children and had just sent their youngest son off to college. She'd worked as a journalist and author for three decades, and she admitted to being tired and ready to slow down.

Brenda soon relented and was surprised by just how much she and Mark enjoyed working through the financial-planning steps. Determined to pay off their debts faster and start saving more for retirement, she and her husband cut back on spending and found extra work.

When Brenda identified her value-driven goals, she realized that she wanted to return to college and earn a master's degree in social work so she could help the disadvantaged. It seemed impossible to her, especially with two children in college. But as she and Mark got a handle on their money, she became inspired and motivated to pursue her goals, no matter the obstacles.

She was prepared to apply to various colleges, but before she could send off the applications, she happened to meet a professor from New York University's Silver School of Social Work. Without prompting, two minutes after meeting Brenda, this woman insisted that she apply to her institution. Brenda did and was soon admitted to the graduate social work program.

New York University is a prestigious and expensive school, but there was little scholarship money available for "mature" students. A financial-aid officer confided to Brenda that one reason she wasn't getting scholarships was that she'd been out of school for thirty-eight years and as undergraduate hadn't done all that well.

Brenda didn't let that discourage her. She went out and found extra writing work, and although it took longer than she'd hoped, she saved enough for the tuition. But before she could start school, her age got in the way.

NYU's graduate social work students are required to work three days full-time as unpaid interns at social-welfare agencies. Brenda was turned down at her first interview, because the supervisor said she needed someone who had the energy to do a lot of running around. Brenda insisted that she had plenty of energy and offered to go home and return with copies of some of the books she'd written. The woman told her not to break her neck getting back to her. It took another two interviews before Brenda found an agency that welcomed her.

When school and work began, she heard so many jokes and comments about age that they wore her down. She says she started wondering whether her critics had been right—maybe she was too old to manage her new responsibilities. In addition to the internship, she had to attend school full-time, complete twenty to twenty-five hours a week of homework, sustain a twenty-two-year marriage, and spend four days a week writing this book. She managed it all by praying, working every day of the week—including holidays—and sleeping four to five hours a night. But she felt happier than she could remember. She not only earned straight As, but she was also selected for a prestigious paid internship and was awarded two scholarships, which paid her second year of tuition.

Brenda told me, "It's like you always say, Aaron. It's not just about money. When you're worried about how you can survive in the future, you keep your head down; you're afraid to look up. Financial literacy allows you to shift your gaze, and that's when you realize how much of the world you've been missing. I used to tell my kids that I was going to die by the time I was sixty-one. That was fear talking. I was afraid of running out of money. And fear can control your behavior. I ate as if I wanted to make early death a reality. My diet has changed, along with so much else. . . . I have reenvisioned my life."

Now it's your turn. You might not have gotten as far as you'd like with financial planning. You might want to turn to the first page of this book and start again. I'm imagining that you still have a way to go, but I am certain that you can get there.

If you're searching for answers about what to do with the rest of your life, prayer can always help you see more clearly.

You'll find that when you're no longer consumed with worry about money, you will shift away from activities of self-interest and develop a larger vision of service that is tied to the common good. You can then find a vocation that will allow you to express moral and spiritual purpose. Wherever you are and whatever you're doing, I challenge you to empower your money, so you can find a sense of vocation built upon the vision of God, who out of love creates, and through his vision came into this world as a servant.

What gifts and strengths have you identified in this work that will help you forge a secure hold on the future? You might want to record them in the space provided:

_____

_____

_____

_____

_____

_____

When you reflect upon these gifts, remember the words of Luke 12:48: "From everyone to whom much has been given, much will be required; and from one to whom much has been entrusted, even more will be demanded."

When I write about envisioning the future, I'm referring to inner vision. That's why I considered it quite significant that just as Brenda and I were finishing this work, as part of her social work intern responsibilities, she visited a client on behalf of her agency. Mrs. M, a ninety-eight-year-old African American woman, was too frail to walk downstairs one last time to feel the sun. She has no family. She is blind and her face is disfigured from botched surgery. Brenda didn't know what to expect when she entered Mrs. M's well-worn apartment, but she wasn't prepared for what she saw.

This frail blind woman answered the door praising the Lord. Brenda had come to see how Mrs. M was doing, but she almost forgot to ask. Mrs. M's spirit served as testimony to God's mercy and grace. Brenda knew immediately that she was in the presence of a truly wise woman. During their visit, Mrs. M. began to pray. Struggling to her feet, she gripped Brenda's hand with strength that belied her frailty and commenced talking to the Lord. Brenda silently asked God for a message that she could share with you—all of you who are reading this book—to help you continue in your journey.

Mrs. M looked up through unseeing eyes and said in a firm, clear voice: "The Lord is always listening for you to talk to him. He may not come when you want him, but he's a timely God. He's never late, and he's right on time."

I started this book by explaining that it's not too late to make a change for the better. Please keep Mrs. M's words in mind. You are not alone. This is your time. This is your life. Live it well.

Appendix

Worksheets for Tracking Your Expenses

PERSONAL AND FAMILY EXPENSES

Category	Current	Increase or Decrease Planned?
Books/periodicals		
Care for parents or other extended family		
Child care/after-school programs		
Child's allowance Child support		
Church donations (tithe)		
Dental		

continued

Category	Current	Increase or Decrease Planned?
Eating out		
Education for children (tuition, tutors, books, school supplies, field trips, etc.)		
Education/yours		
Education/spouse		
Groceries		
Hair care/yours		
Hair care/spouse		
Hair care/child's		
Health care: insurance, copays, prescriptions		
Household staples: cleaning products, lightbulbs, etc.		
Laundry/dry cleaning		
Manicure/pedicure		
Pet care		
Phones: Cell Home		

Category	Current	Increase or Decrease Planned?
Public transportation		
Self-improvement		
Vacations		
Miscellaneous		
Unexpected		
Total	$	$

After totaling your weekly expenses, please add them up for the monthly total and then figure out your additional monthly costs:

EXPENSES FOR HOME/OTHER PROPERTY

Category	Increase or Decrease Planned?
Mortgage	
Home-equity loan	
Real estate tax	
Rent payment	

continued

Category	Increase or Decrease Planned?
Home owner's insurance	
Home owner fees	
Electricity	
Gas/oil	
Trash pickup	
Water	
Sewer	
Cable or satellite TV	
Internet	
Unexpected	
Yard and garden care	
Major repair	
Regular repair	
Furniture	
Household help	
Additional real estate	
Other	
Total	$

CAR EXPENSES

Category	Current	Increase or Decrease Planned?
Car loan/lease payment Second-car loan		
Insurance		
Fuel		
Fuel for spouse		
Repairs/maintenance		
Parking, tolls		
Car wash		
Total	$	$

BUSINESS EXPENSES

Category	Current	Increase or Decrease Planned
Bank fees		
Club dues		

continued

Category	Current	Increase or Decrease Planned
Credit card debt		
Office supplies		
Loans		
Miscellaneous		
Post office		
Student loans		
Unreimbursed business		
Total	$	$

TAXES

Category	Current	Increase or Decrease Planned
Your FICA		
Spouse's FICA		
Your Medicare		
Spouse's Medicare		
Your federal income		

Category	Current	Increase or Decrease Planned
Spouse's federal income		
Your state income		
Spouse's state income		
Total	$	$

MONTHLY CONTRIBUTIONS TOWARD INVESTMENTS

Category	Increase or Decrease Planned
Stocks/bonds/mutual funds	
Your life insurance	
Spouse's life insurance	
Other insurance	
401(k)-type retirement fund	
Other financial plans or investments to which you contribute	
Total	$

TOTAL EXPENDITURES

Personal/family	$
Home/other property	$
Car	$
Business	$
Investments	$
Grand total	$

Notes

Introduction

1   **9 million black baby boomers**: Kim Campbell, "The Many Faces of the Baby Boomers," *Christian Science Monitor*, 26 Jan. 2005, www.csmonitor.com/2005/0126/p15s02-lihc.html.

2   **people who did a significant amount**: Penelope Wang, "What Works: Planners Prosper, *Money*, 12 Sept. 2006, http://money.cnn.com/2006/09/07/pf/retirement/retire0610_whatworks_shah.moneymag/index.htm.

2   **Ariel/Schwab 2006 Black Investors Survey**: Ariel Mutual Funds/Charles Schwab & Co., Inc. Black Investor Survey: "Saving and Investing Among Higher Income African-American and White Americans," 22 June 2006, www.arielcapital.com/content/view/643/1173.

3   **local black churches**: Holly Rodriguez, "Giving an Education in Financial Planning: Aaron W. Smith Began Building Client Base from Black Churches," *Richmond Times-Dispatch*, 9 Apr. 2001.

4   **More than 37 million Americans are over sixty-five**: Charles Duhigg, "Six Decades at the Center of Attention, and Counting," ("Week in Review"), *New York Times*, 6 Jan. 2008.

4   **likely to ignore commercials**: Duhigg, "Six Decades."

4   **consumers look to loved ones**: "Word-of-Mouth the Most Powerful Selling Tool," Nielsen Global Survey, 1 Oct. 2007, www.nielsen.com/media/2007/pro71001.html.

7   **people were quizzed on simple calculations**: Wang, "What Works."

8   **Black American economic buying power**: Amadu Kaba, "The Gradual Shift of Wealth and Power from African American Males to

African American Females," *Journal of African American Studies* 9 (Winter 2005): 3.

8   **black buying power is expected to reach**: "African-American TV Usage and Buying Power," Nielsen Company, 18 Oct. 2007, www.nielsen.com/media/2007/pr_071018a.html.

9   **Some financial advisers are essentially salespeople**: Charles Duhigg, "For Elderly Investors, Instant Experts Abound," *New York Times*, 8 July 2007.

Chapter 1: Defining Your Values

20   **Allstate Insurance asked**: "What Americans Fear, Fourth Annual Allstate 'Reality Check Survey,'" http://media.allstate.com/categories/41-2004/releases/4251-pennies-saved-today-earn.

24   **study of men who had unhappy childhoods**: G. Valiant, A. C. DiRago, Ken Mukamal, "Natural History of Male Psychological Health, XV: Retirement Satisfaction," *American Journal of Psychiatry*, 163(4), April 2006, pp. 682–688.

25   **studies suggest that contentment-inducing activities**: John Stossel and Sylvia Johnson, "Doing Good, and Feeling Better," *20/20*, ABC News, 20 Aug. 2007. http://abcnews.go.com/2020/story?id=2685717.

Chapter 2: Getting Your Goals Straight

31   **People with financial goals have twice the wealth**: Walecia Konrad, "Avoid These Money Traps," *AARP*, July & Aug. 2007, 40.

37   **Dr. Harriet P. McAdoo credits the kinship system**: A. O. Harrison et al., "Family Ecologies of Ethnic Minority Children," *Child Development* 61 (1990): 347–62.

37   **27 percent of African Americans polled have adults**: Ariel Mutual Funds/Charles Schwab & Co., Inc. Black Investor Survey: "Saving and Investing Among Higher Income African-American and White Americans," 22 June 2006, www.arielcapital.com/content/view/643/1173.

37   **on average people pay about $5,500 annually**: Jane Gross, "Study Finds Higher Outlays for Caregivers of Older Relatives," *New York Times*, 19 Nov. 2007.

Chapter 3: Facing Reality and Exploring Your Dreams

49   **the most optimistic people on earth**: Economic World Bank, "Africa Most Optimistic Region for 2006: Global Poll," econ.worldbank.org/WBSITE/EXTERNAL/EXTDEC/EXTRESEARCH/EXTPROGRAMS/EXTTRADERESEARCH/0,,contentMDK:20773479.

Chapter 5: Paying Yourself First

67   **50 percent of black women raising children**: Amadu Kaba, "The Gradual Shift of Wealth and Power from African American Males to African American Females," *Journal of African American Studies*, 9 (Winter 2005): 3.

71   **trend toward greater savings among African Americans**: Wilhelmina A. Leigh and Danielle Huff, "Retirement Prospects and Perils: Public Opinion on Social Security and Wealth, by Race 1997–2005," Joint Center for Political and Economic Studies, 2 Apr. 2007, www.jointcenter .org/index.php/current_research_and_policy_activities/economic_ad vancement/social_security_african_americans/inadequate_personal_ savings_demonstrates_the_need_for_social_security.

71   **AARP Foundation Women's Leadership Circle Study**: Jean Kalata, AARP Project Manager, "Looking at Act II of Women's Lives: Thriving & Striving from 45 On," *AARP*, Apr. 2006, www.aarp.org/research/hous ing-mobility/indliving/wlcresearch.html.

75   **A 2007 Charles Schwab study**: Associated Press, "Investors Ignoring the Often Free Advice of 401(k) Providers Can See Their Returns Suffer," *San Jose Mercury News*, 27, Nov. 2007, www.mercurynews.com/ personalfinance/ci_7572088.

78   **Don't dip into retirement savings**: Jane Bennett Clark, "How to Cover the College Bills," *Kiplinger's Step-By-Step Advice for Every Age*, Winter 2007: 80.

Chapter 6: Getting a Handle on Your Spending

85   **38 percent of married adults**: "What Americans Pay for—and How," Pew Research Center study, 7 Feb. 2007, http://pewsocialtrends.org/ pubs/407/what-americans-pay-for—and-how.

Chapter 7: Paying Down Debt

97   **cut up his credit card on the spot**: Jeffrey Toobin, "Unforgiven," *New Yorker*, 12 Nov. 2007, 86.

98   **non-mortgage debts**: John Leland, "Turning to Churches or Scripture to Cope with Debt," *New York Times*, 29 Apr. 2007.

102   **79 percent of credit reports contained errors**: Tanisha A. Sykes, *Black Enterprise*, July 2005, http://find articles.com/p/articles/mi_m1365/ is_12_35/ai_n15652756looksmart.

102   **25 percent contained errors that could**: Sandra Block, "Fixing Errors in Credit Report Is No Small Task," *USA Today*, 27 Sept. 2005, www .usatoday.com/money/perfi/credit/2005-09-27-credit-report-usat_ x.htm.

Chapter 8: Maximizing Your Cash

115 **Zhang Yin of China:** David Barboza, "Blazing a Paper Trail in China," 16 Jan. 2007, *New York Times*, www.nytimes.com/2007/01/16/business/16trash.html.

115 **Corey Kossack of Arizona:** Tony Natale, "ebay Fertile Ground for Young Entrepreneur," *East Valley* (Mesa, Ariz.) *Tribune*, 27 May 2007, www.eastvalleytribune.com/story/90497.

117 **Retirement Savings Contribution Tax Credit:** Mary Beth Franklin, "Give Yourself Extra Credit," *Kiplinger's*, July 2006, www.kiplinger.com/magazine/archives/2006/07/taxcredit.html.

Chapter 9: Pinpointing the Amount You Need to Retire

119 **half of this country's prison inmates:** Orlando Patterson, "Jena, O. J. and the Jailing of Black America," *New York Times*, 30 Sept. 2007, www.nytimes.com/2007/09/30/opinion/30patterson.html.

120 **white males with criminal records:** Jennifer Greenstein Altmann, "Sociologist Studies Lasting Confines of Imprisonment," *Princeton Weekly Bulletin* 94 (8 Nov. 2004): 9, www.princeton.edu/pr/pwb/04/1108/1b.shtml.

Chapter 10: Knowing When to Take Social Security

137 **They had been shut out of Social Security:** Pierre Epstein, *Abraham Epstein: The Forgotten Father of Social Security* (Columbia: University of Missouri Press, 2005), 162.

138 **some White House advisers wanted:** Ira Katznelson, *When Affirmative Action Was White: An Untold History of Racial Inequality in Twentieth-Century America* (New York: W. W. Norton, 2005), 22, 44.

139 **helped millions of black elders:** Wilhelmina A. Leigh and Danielle Huff, Joint Center for Political and Economic Studies, "Retirement Prospects and Perils: Public Opinion on Social Security and Wealth, by Race 1997–2005, 2 Apr. 2007," www.jointcenter.org/publications_recent_publications/social_policy/public_opinion_on_social_security_and_wealth_byrace_1997_2005full_report; and address by AARP board member Jose Maldonado at the Mexican National Institute for Older Persons International Conference of Aging on 3 Nov. 2005, www.aarp.org/research/international/speeches/nov3_05_jmaldonado.html.

139 **Forty percent of African Americans sixty-five and older:** Ke Bin Wu, "African Americans Age 65 and Older: Their Sources of Income," Fact Sheet, AARP Public Policy Institute, 5 Sept. 2004, www.aarp.org/research/reference/minorities/aresearch-import-906-FS100.html.

139 **Elderly black women**: Kilolo Kijakazi and Wendell Primus, "Options for Reducing Poverty Among Elderly Women by Improving Supplemental Security Income," National Academy of Social Insurance 12th Annual Conference, 27 Jan. 2000, www.cbpp.org/1-27-00soc sec.htm.

139 **would have more than doubled**: Kilolo Kijakazi, "GAO Report Shows Social Security Is Favorable to People of Color but Some Changes in It Could Harm Minority Communities," Center on Budget and Policy Priorities, 12 May 2003, www.cbpp.org/5-12-03socsec.htm.

139 **Federal Reserve chairman Alan Greenspan**: Associated Press, "Greenspan's Social Security Alarm," 27 Aug. 2004, *CBSNews.com*, www.cbsnews.com/stories/2004/08/27/national/main638921.shtml.

139 **President George W. Bush soon proposed**: "Bush Moves to Privatize Social Security," *USA Today*, 10 Nov. 2004, www.usatoday.com/news/washington/2004-11-10-social-security_x.htm-55k.

140 **sea change in African American views**: Leigh and Huff, "Retirement Prospects and Perils."

142 **the number of people eighty-five and older increased**: "The 65 and Over Population, 2000," U.S. Department of Commerce, Oct. 2001, www.census.gov/prod/2001pubs/c2kbr01.10.

142 **Social Security isn't increased immediately**: Penelope Wang, "Time to Get Real," *Money*, Nov. 2007, 89.

143 **low-income individuals receive more**: Ibid.

144 **Hugh Price and Julian Bond pointed out**: Hugh Price and Julian Bond, "Social Security's Stable Benefit," *New York Times*, 26 July 2001, http://query.nytimes.com/gst/fullpage.html?res=9C0CE2D7163D F935A15754C0A9679C8B63.

147 **provide the most possible for the surviving spouse**: Mary Beth Franklin, "Choose Your Date," *Kiplinger.com*, Oct. 2006, www.kiplinger.com/magazine/archives/2006/10/retired4.html.

Chapter 11: Choosing Traditional or Roth IRAs

153 **IBM, Lockheed Martin, General Motors**: Daniel Gross, "The Big Freeze," *AARP Bulletin*, Mar. 2006, www.aarp.org/bulletin/yourmoney/big_freeze.html.

153 **decline in the prevalence of DB**: Pat Regnier, "Make Your Money Last Long and Prosper," *Money*, Oct. 2006, 98–99.

153 **African American men receiving pensions**: Ke Bin Wu, "African Americans Age 65 and Older: Their Sources of Income," Fact Sheet, AARP Public Policy Institute, Sept. 2004, www.aarp.org/research/reference/minorities/aresearch-import-906-FS100.html.

153 **two thirds of black participants**: Ariel Mutual Funds/Charles Schwab & Co., Inc. Black Investor Survey: "Saving and Investing Among Higher Income African-American and White Americans," 22 June 2006, www.arielcapital.com/content/view/643/1173.

161 **President Gerald Ford**: James A. Wooten, *The Employee Retirement Income Security Act of 1974: A Political History* (Berkeley: University of California Press, 2005), 1–2.

Chapter 12: Recognizing an Annuity for What It Is

165 **a third of current retirees**: "Study of Older Americans Finds Retirement More a 'State' Than a 'Date,'" 3 Apr. 2006, MetLife study, *Senior Journal.com*, www.seniorjournal.com. http://seniorjournal.com/NEWS/Retirement/6-4-03/studyofolderAmericans.htm.

170 **male life expectancy**: Stephen Ohlemacher, "U.S. Lags Behind 41 Nations in Life Span," *Boston Globe*, 11 Aug. 2007, www.boston.com/news/education/higher/articles/2007/08/11/us_life_span_shorter.

175 **exploitation of the elderly involve annuity sales**: Charles Duhigg, "For Elderly Investors, Instant Experts Abound," *New York Times*, 8 July 2007, www.nytimes.com/2007/07/08/business/08advisor.html?pagewanted=1&_r=1.

Chapter 13: Understanding Our Passion for Real Estate

181 **2005 article in the** *Journal of Blacks in Higher Education*: T. Cross and R. B. Slater, "Black Student College Graduation Rates Remain Low, but Modest Progress Begins to Show," *Journal of Blacks in Higher Education*, Winter 2008, www.jbhe.com/features/50_blackstudent_gradrates.html.

182 **put a lot of trust in real estate**: Ariel/Schwab 2006 Black Investors Survey.

183 **less than 43 percent of African Americans**: Haya El Naser, "Blacks a Growing Part of Retirement Migration South, *USA Today*, 7 Dec. 2005, www.usatoday.com/news/nation/2005-12-07-black-retirees_x.htm.

184 **trade surplus of $1 trillion**: Steve Schifferes, "China's Trillion Dollar Surplus," British Broadcasting Corporation, 2 Nov. 2006, http://news.bbc.co.uk/1/hi/business/6106280.stm.

184 **loans without proof of employment**: Vikas Bajaj and Jenny Anderson, "Inquiry Focuses on Withholding of Data on Loans," *New York Times*, 12 Jan. 2008.

184 **Subprime loans don't always lead**: David Brooks, "Two Cheers for Wall St., *New York Times*, 25 Jan. 2008.

185 **Predatory brokers and lenders concentrated**: Vikas Bajaj and Ford

Fessenden, "The Subprime Landscape, from Detroit to Ithaca: What's Behind the Race Gap?," *New York Times*, 4 Nov. 2007.

186 **New York University's Furman Center**: Manny Fernandez, "Racial Disparity Found Among New Yorkers with High-Rate Mortgages," *New York Times*, 15 Oct. 2007.

186 **Ted Janusz**: Description of the author and his practices from Amazon .com, www.amazon.com/Kickback-Confessions-Mortgage-Ted-Janusz/ dp/1600130011.

186 **incentive for local financial institutions**: Liam Pleven and Susanne Craig, "Deal Fees Under Fire Amid Mortgage Crisis," *Wall Street Journal*, 17 Jan. 2008.

186 **private well-established firms**: Ibid.

187 **Federal Reserve governor warned**: Edmund L. Andrews, "Fed and Regulators Shrugged As the Subprime Crisis Spread," *New York Times*, 18 Dec. 2007.

187 **insane greed ruled the day**: Ben Stein, "It's Time to Act Like Grown-Ups, *New York Times*, 11 Nov. 2007.

187 **to as high as 15 percent**: Jane Bryant Quinn, "Maybe We Can Work It Out," *Newsweek*, 26 Nov. 2007, 94.

187 **home owners who fell dangerously behind**: Chris Isidore, *CNN Money.com.*, 6 Dec. 2007, http://money.cnn.com/2007/12/06/real_estate/ foreclosure_delinquencies/index.htm.

187 **Foreclosures rose to almost 2 million**: Walecia Konrad, "How to Ride Out a Recession," *AARP*, March & Apr. 2008, 38.

187 **"forty acres and a mule"**: Quintard Taylor, "Forty Acres and a Mule," *Blackpast.org*, www.blackpast.com/?q=aah/forty-acres-and-mule.

188 **discriminated blatantly against African Americans**: Adam Gordon, "The Creation of Homeownership: How New Deal Changes in Banking Regulation Simultaneously Made Homeownership Accessible to Whites and Out of Reach for Blacks," *Yale Law Journal* 115 (Oct. 2005), 1: 186–226.

188 **more than one million African Americans served**: Kevin Chappell, "Blacks in World War II" *Ebony*, Sept. 1995, http://findarticles .com/p/articles/mi_m1077/is_n11_v50/ai_17362103.

189 **GI Bill benefits fueled a housing boom**: William Celis 3d, "50 Years Later, the Value of the G.I. Bill Is Questioned," *New York Times*, 22 June 1994, http://query.nytimes.com/gst/fullpage.html?res=9807E6DC103D F931A15755C0A962958260.

189 **did not benefit from housing assistance**: Ira Katznelson, *When Affirmative Action Was White? An Untold History of Racial Inequality in Twentieth-Century America* (New York: W. W. Norton, 2005), 177–178.

190 **"reverse redlining"**: Libby Lewis, "Baltimore Blames Lender for

Wave of Foreclosures," National Public Radio, 11 Jan. 2008, www.npr
.org/templates/story/story.php?storyId=17994964.

190 **estimated 15 to 50 percent of the subprime loans**: Les Christie,
"Wow, I Could've Had a Prime Mortgage," *CNNMoney.com*. 30 May 2007,
http://money.cnn.com/2007/05/29/real_estate/could_have_had_a_
prime/index.htm.

191 **Home ownership can help you feel invested**: Kate Ashford, "Happiness after health: Should We Buy or Should We Rent?" *Money*, Oct.
2006, 70.

Chapter 15: Making Wall Street Work for You

219 **New York University's Stern School**: Annual Returns on Stock,
T.Bonds and T.Bills: 1928–Current," http://pages.stern.nyu.edu/~adam
odar/New_Home_Page/datafile/histretSP.html.

219 **black participation rate dipped to 57 percent**: Mellody Hobson,
"Total Return, Retirement in Black and White," *Black Enterprise*, Jan.
2008, 35.

Chapter 16: Selecting Insurance That
Fits Your Needs

236 **evidence suggested that**: Associated Press, "Insurance Industry Face
Lawsuits After Century of Race-Based Charges," *USA Today*, 9 Oct. 2004,
www.usatoday.com/news/nation/2004-10-09-race-based-insurance_x
.htm; and Kenneth N. Gilpin, "Settlement Near for Insurer Accused of
Overcharging Blacks," *New York Times*, 10 Jan. 2002, http://query.ny
times.com/gst/fullpage.html?res=9C03E0DE1039F933A25752C0A
9649C8B63.

240 **burial policies are costlier**: Erik Eckholm, "Burial Insurance Provides Peace of Mind for $2 a Week," *New York Times*, 3 Dec. 2006.

241 **people without coverage were found to suffer**: "No Insurance,
Poor Health," editorial, *New York Times*, 3 Jan. 2008.

241 **Commonwealth Fund survey**: Hispanic and African American
Adults Are Uninsured at Rates One-and-a-Half to Three Times Higher
Than White Adults, 1 Aug. 2006, www.commonwealthfund.org/news
room/newsroom_show.htm?doc_id=386212.

241 **health-care costs rising**: Milt Freudeneim, "Health Care Costs Rise
Twice as Much as Inflation," *New York Times*, 27 Sept. 2007.

241 **had health insurance**: Judy Foreman, "High Medical Bills Don't Have
to Lead to Bankruptcy," *Boston Globe*, 22 Feb. 2005, www.boston.com/
business/articles/2005/02/22/high_medical_bills_donthave_to_lead_
to_bankruptcy.

242   **credit card balances nearly $3,700 higher**: Christopher Rowland, "Patients Piling Medical Costs on Credit Cards," *Boston Globe*, 22 Jan. 2007, www.boston.com/business/globe/articles/2007/01/22/patients_piling_medical_costs_on_credit_cards.

243   **Consider temporary health insurance**: Jean Chatzky, "Cover Yourself," *Time*, 21 Apr. 2003, www.time.com/time/magazine/article/0,9171,1004694,00.html.

248   **more than 500,000 LTC policies**: Cybele Weisser, "Afford the Care You Need," *CNNMoney.com*, Oct. 2006, http://money.cnn.com/2006/09/11/pf/retirement/retire0610_ltcare.moneymag/index.htm.